Sexual Harassment in Employment

SEXUAL HARASSMENT IN EMPLOYMENT

by Susan M. Omilian

Callaghan

CALLAGHAN & COMPANY
3201 Old Glenview Road
Wilmette, Illinois 60091

Library of Congress Cataloging-in-Publication Data

Omilian, Susan M.
Sexual harassment in employment / by Susan M. Omilian.
p. cm.
Includes index.
ISBN 0-8366-0013-4 (pbk.)
1. Sex discrimination in employment—Law and legislation—United States. 2. Sexual harassment of women—Law and legislation—United States. I. Title.
KF3467.05 1987
344.73'014133—dc 19
[347.30414133] 87-24593
CIP

For D.G.
The perfect book widow
with love and thanks

Contents

Sexual Harassment in Employment

CHAPTER ONE

Introduction: The Theory of a Sexual Harassment Case

§1:01. Overview.

A single sentence made history on June 19, 1986, when Justice William H. Rehnquist penned for a unanimous U.S. Supreme Court: "Without question, when a supervisor sexually harasses a subordinate because of a subordinate's sex, that supervisor discriminates on the basis of sex."[1]

It was historic because it was the first time the Supreme Court had ruled on the viability of a legal cause of action for sexual harassment claims under Title VII of the Civil Rights Act of 1964.[2] But the pronouncement was also anti-climactic. For almost ten years previously, the lower federal courts had been holding that sexual harassment was an illegal workplace practice, beginning in 1976 with the decision in *Williams v. Saxbe.*[3]

Then too, this declaration in *Meritor Savings Bank* was almost inconspicuous in the decision. The Justices, in both the majority and concurring opinions, merely used it as a preliminary fact in a heated discussion of several important legal questions raised by the facts of the case. Some of their questions are in fact, the most pressing issues in sexual harassment litigation today. They include:

Does Title VII prohibit sexual harassment that creates an "intimidating, hostile or offensive work environment" absent a tangible job detriment? Is an employer strictly liable when a supervisor's actions create such an environment? What if the plaintiff had previously consented to the sexual demands? How does a court determine if a sexual advance is "unwelcomed?" Can an employer avoid liability by having a company policy against sexual harassment? Is the plaintiff's manner of dress or "sexual fantasies" relevant?

This book explores these questions and the many others that await an attorney representing a plaintiff or defending an employer in a sexual harassment case. Chapters will be dedicated to the development of Title VII law since 1976 and since the Supreme Court's decision in *Meritor Savings Bank.* But the book will also look at other causes of action which bolster a Title VII lawsuit, such as state tort actions, constitutional challenges and contract rights or those which provide a claim for workers compensation or unemployment benefits. Also discussed will be special litigation issues in sexual harassment cases, such as the admissibility of the plaintiff's prior sexual history and possible defenses for employer in a sexual harassment case that may actually help prevent sexual harassment in the workplace.

FOOTNOTES

[1] *Meritor Savings Bank v. Vinson,*—U.S.—, 106 S.Ct. 2399, 2404, 40 FEP Cases 1822, 54 LW 4703 (1986).

[2] (Section 701 *et. seq.,* as amended 42 U.S.C. Section 2000e *et. seq.*).

[3] 413 F. Supp. 654 (D.D.C. 1976).

§1:02. Early Cases.

Before tackling the specifics of a sexual harassment case, it is important to examine the broader legal theory that underlies *Meritor Savings Bank* and many of the sexual harassment cases that have been litigated in the past decade. It is fascinating to see how a legal theory of sex discrimination first came to be applied to sexual harassment cases under the Title VII "sex-plus" legal analysis. Also interesting is how other Title VII legal analysis was adopted to fit novel fact patterns of sexual harassment that arose later. But in the application of theory to facts, it is important to observe the basic underlying assumptions that are made about men and women in our society. For decisions in future sexual harassment cases will be shaped and analyzed by the principles that have evolved from applying a theory of discrimination that sees women and men in a one way but not another.

To begin with, the federal courts were not receptive to the idea that sexual harassment constituted a cause of action under Title VII. In the earliest decided case, the U.S. District Court for the District of Columbia found in *Barnes v. Train*[1] that "the substance of plaintiff's complaint was that she was discriminated against not because she was a woman but because she refused to engage in a sexual affair with her supervisor."[2] (*Barnes* was the first sexual harassment case decided by a federal court; however, it was not reported until approximately two years later.) A year later, the court in *Corne v. Bausch & Lomb*[3] ruled, in the first reported case, that the alleged sexual harassment was merely a matter of the "personal proclivity, peculiarity or mannerism" of the male supervisor and nothing in Title VII prohibits verbal and physical advances where the conduct has "no relationship to the nature of the employment."[4]

Similarly, the court in *Miller v. Bank of America*[5] held that the plaintiff had alleged "essentially the isolated and unauthorized sex misconduct of one employee to another," and not an injury actionable under Title VII. Finally, in *Tomkins v. Public Service Elec. & Gas Co.*[6] the district court ruled that "If the plaintiff's view were to prevail, no superior could prudently attempt to open a social dialogue with any subordinate of either sex. An invitation to dinner could become an invitation to a federal lawsuit if a once harmonious relationship turned sour at some later time."[7]

In these decisions, the courts did not grasp how the plaintiffs' allegations of sexual harassment moved beyond the personal to expose a serious, pervasive problem for working women which was based on sex discrimination. They also did not see how they could have provided relief by applying an established Title VII legal analysis to the cases.

FOOTNOTES

[1] 13 FEP Cases 123 (D. D.C. 1974).
[2] *Id.* at 124.
[3] 390 F. Supp. 161, 10 FEP Cases 289 (D.C. Ariz. 1975).
[4] *Id.* at 163.
[5] 418 F. Supp. 233, 234, 13 FEP Cases 439 (N.D. Cal. 1976).
[6] 422 F. Supp. 553 (D.C. N.J. 1976).
[7] *Id.* at 557.

§1:03. Application of Title VII.

Title VII relief was to be accomplished by the district court in *Williams v. Saxbe* in April, 1976, and in July, 1977, by the appellate court in *Barnes v. Costle.*[1] Both courts rebutted the *Corne* rationale that sexual harassment was not discrimination based on sex by finding that, although both sexes could be sexually propositioned, it was not necessary for the characteristic (here of "sexual attractiveness") to be peculiar to women in order for sexual harassment to be illegal under Title VII. In so deciding, the courts relied on the "sex-plus" analysis in *Sprogis v. United Air Lines, Inc.*[2] and *Phillips v. Martin Marietta Corp.*[3] In *Martin Marietta,* a company policy allowed men to be hired who had preschool children but not women. *Sprogis* involved a "no-marriage" rule which was applied to female stewardesses only. In both cases, since women were not only discriminated against because they were women but also because they were parents or married, the courts found that this was discrimination based on a classification (sex) prohibited by Title VII *plus* one other factor (e.g. married or parents) which is not a prohibited classification. The "no-hire" and "no-marriage" policies were discriminatory because they were applied to only women, even though men were similarly situated in that they could also be married or have children.

Applying this "sex-plus" rule to sexual harassment cases, the

Williams and *Barnes* courts found that "sexual attractiveness" was a "plus" characteristic like marriage in *Sprogis* and/or parenthood in *Martin Marietta*. Although this characteristic of sexual attractiveness was not peculiar to the female sex, nonetheless allegations that females only were required to accede to sexual demands did state a cause of action under the "sex-plus" analysis. The *Barnes* court added that

> . . . the objectionable employment condition embraces something more than the employee's gender but the fact remains that gender was also involved to a significant degree. For while some but not all employees of one sex were subjected to the condition, no employee of the opposite sex was affected.[4]

It is significant that in scrutinizing the facts in *Barnes* under this sex-plus analysis, the court noted that no employees of the opposite sex (men) were affected. Initially, some legal commentators feared that this meant the legal theory of sexual discrimination being applied here was contingent upon only women being the victims of sexual harassment. One commentator wrote:

> . . . [T]o disallow a claim of discrimination on the ground that *someday, somewhere,* the roles may be reversed would effectively ban all discrimination suits from the court. Blacks may discriminate against whites, but this does not prevent courts from finding discrimination against blacks unlawful.[5]

Subsequently however, males have been able to sustain claims of sexual harassment against female supervisors under Title VII.[6] Homosexual advances have also been found to be within the purview of Title VII.[7]

Footnotes

1 561 F.2d 983, 15 FEP Cases 345 (D.C. Cir. 1977), *reversing and remanding Barnes v. Train* 13 FEP Cases 123 (D.D.C. 1974).

2 444 F.2d 1194 (7th Cir. 1971).

3 400 U.S. 542, 91 S.Ct. 496, 27 L.Ed.2d 613 (1971).

4 561 F.2d 983, at 991–992.

5 Comment, "Title VII: Legal Protection Against Sexual Harassment," 53 WASH LAW REV. 123, 152 (1977).

[6] *Huebschen v. Dept. of Health,* 547 F. Supp. 1168, 32 FEP Cases 1521 (D.C. Wisc. 1982) *reversed on other grounds,* 716 F.2d 1167, 32 FEP Cases 1582 (7th Cir. 1983).

[7] *Wright v. Methodist Youth Services, Inc.,* 551 F. Supp. 307, 25 FEP Cases 563 (N.D. Ill. 1981); *Joyner v. AAA Cooper Transportation,* 597 F. Supp. 537, 36 FEP Cases 1644 (M.D. Ala. 1983).

§1:04. Sexual Harassment of Men and Women.

Beyond a role reversal in a sexual harassment case, the courts have been fascinated with the possibility that males and females both could be harassed by the same bisexual supervisor or by separate incidents in the same workplace. Then, the courts have cautioned, the sexual harassment is not discrimination, just inappropriate, distasteful behavior applied to both sexes equally. The warning first appeared in *Barnes,* as a footnote in the appellate court decision which read, "In the case of the bisexual supervisor, the insistence upon sexual favors would not constitute gender discrimination because it would apply to male and female employees alike."[1] To date, no employer in a reported decision has defended a sexual harassment case by admitting that individuals of both sexes are harassed equally in their workplace! If conceivable, the tragedy of such a situation would be that, as a commentator has put it, ". . . only the discriminatory application is being attacked, not the evil itself."[2]

Footnotes

[1] *Barnes v. Costle*, 561 F.2d 983, 990 (D.C. Cir. 1977), note 55.

[2] 53 WASH. LAW REV. 123 at 136, n. 62.

§1:05. The "Differences" Approach.

It is instructive to think about the improbable scenario described in the preceeding section because it exposes the underlying assumption in the theory of sex discrimination applied to sexual harassment cases that women and men are equal until some well-founded difference shows up, like the sexual propositioning of one sex but not the other. While that assumption appears magnanimous, it flaws this theory of discrimination in its application. Catharine A. MacKinnon in her book, *Sexual Harassment of Working Women,*[1] examines the dilemma of this theory of sex discrimination which she labels the "differences" approach.

> The differences approach . . . begins with the usually unarticulated notion that social equality means that equals should be treated equally. This means that people who are the same should be treated the same.[2]

She continues:

> A differentiation is based on sex when it can be shown that a person of the opposite sex in the same position is not treated the same. This requires that the person of the opposite sex be in a comparable position.[3]

For MacKinnon, a clear example of the differences approach is, of course, *Phillips v. Martin Marietta,* discussed above, for the employer was prohibited from having one hiring policy for women and another for men, while both sexes were similarly situated with pre-school children. MacKinnon finds the epitomy of the differences approach in *Gilbert v. General Electric*[4] where the Supreme Court decided that discrimination on the basis of pregnancy was *not* discrimination on the basis of sex. There, the Court found a reason to differentiate between the sexes because, as only women could get pregnant, a person of the opposite sex—a man—was not in a comparable position.

This approach to discrimination theory, then, is limited both by its preliminary assumption that both sexes are equal and by its focus on finding differences which would eliminate the discrimination. Without comparability (as in *Gilbert*) or lack of differences (which usually means women and men are treated equally as bad), the theory unravels. Yet, in reality, most would agree that the law should prohibit sexual harassment even if it is applied to both sexes and many legal commentators vehemently criticized the Court's decision in *Gilbert.* Congress, in fact, passed the Pregnancy Discrimination Amendment[5] to Title VII, specifically to overturn the Court's decision in *Gilbert.*

FOOTNOTES

[1] MacKinnon, *Sexual Harassment of Working Women,* Yale University Press (1979).

[2] MacKinnon, at 107.

[3] *Id.*

[4] 429 U.S. 125, 97 S. Ct. 401, 50 L.Ed.2d 343, 13 FEP Cases 1657 (1976).

[5] 42 U.S.C. Section 2000e(k) (1983).

§1:06. The Inequality Theory.

There is another approach says author Catharine MacKinnon, which she labels the "inequality" view. This approach, she says, more accurately reflects the reality of the workplace where women are more likely to be subordinates and to be sexually harassed. It also recognizes that women are relegated to a secondary social status. MacKinnon writes:

> This approach to inequality is marked by the understanding that sex discrimination is a system that defines women as inferior from men, that cumulatively disadvantages women for their differences from men, as well as ignores their similarities.[1]

She continues:

> A rule or practice is discrimination in the inequality approach if it participates in the systematic social deprivation of one sex because of sex.[2]

For MacKinnon, the logic of the inequality approach is that it requires no comparability of situation between the two sexes, only that a rule or practice like sexual harassment "disportionately burdens one sex because of sex."[3] She explains that under the facts of *Martin Marietta,* if the court had found that family obligations presented a greater job conflict for mothers than for fathers of preschool children, then men and women under the "differences" approach would be different and there would be no sex discrimination. But with the "inequality" view, the differential hiring rule would still have been discriminatory "because it would reinforce the traditionally disportionate burden for parenthood on women."[4]

But the inequality view of sex discrimination has not been adopted in sexual harassment cases to date, including *Meritor Savings Bank.* In fact, a court decision which followed *Meritor Savings Bank* recently reminded us:

> It is of significance to note that instances of complained of sexual conduct that prove equally offensive to male and female workers would not support a Title VII sexual harassment charge because both men and women were accorded like treatment.[5]

In addition to being a reminder of the footnote in *Barnes,* this statement in *Rabidue* means an extension of the underlying assumption in the "differences" approach (that both sexes are equal unless a difference appears) from the sex-plus analysis in *Barnes,* to another legal analysis of sexual harassment which the court used in *Rabidue.*

Footnotes

[1] MacKinnon, *Sexual Harassment of Working Women*, Yale University Press (1979), at 116.

[2] *Id.*

[3] *Id.* at 225.

[4] *Id.*

[5] *Rabidue v. Osceola Refining Co.*, 42 FEP Cases 631, 637 (6th Cir. 1986).

§1:07. The Environment Theory.

This analysis first appeared in *Bundy v. Jackson*[1] where the court faced novel factual allegations unlike those in *Barnes,* described above, where the plaintiff alleged that she was retaliated against because she declined the sexual advances of her supervisor. The plaintiff in *Bundy* claimed that she was subjected to an "intimidating, hostile and offensive work environment," because her workplace was charged with stereotyped sexual insults and propositioning, but she suffered no tangible job detriment (e.g. she was not fired, demoted or retaliated against) as a result of the sexual harassment.

The *Bundy* court found that these allegations did state a cause of action under Title VII by adopting a legal analysis from *Rogers v. EEOC*.[2] There, the plaintiff alleged that her employer, a firm of opticians, by giving unequal service to its Hispanic clients, created a discriminatory and offensive work environment for its Hispanic employees. Judge Goldberg found that such a practice violated Title VII because its language prohibits discrimination in the "terms, conditions or privileges of employment," a phrase which the court found:

> . . . is an expansive concept which sweeps within its protective ambit the practice of creating a work environment heavily charged with ethnic or racial discrimination.[3]

In line with the court's decision in *Rogers v. EEOC*, the *Bundy* court ruled that the "sexually stereotyped insults and demeaning propositions" impinged upon the "psychological and emotional work environment," illegally poisoning that environment in violation of Title VII.[4] This analysis was affirmed by the Supreme Court in *Meritor Savings Bank* where the plaintiff also alleged a hostile, offensive work environment was created as a result of sexual harassment.

While this analysis of sexual harassment is different from the sex-plus analysis, it too seems to rest on the underlying assumption of the "differences" approach, according to the *Rabidue* court, that there is only discrimination if there are differences between sexes that are equal otherwise. But that is not to say that the "inequality" view of sex discrimination is not present in the *Rabidue* decision. In fact, the decision illustrates quite strikingly the two different approaches.

The majority of the three-judge Sixth Circuit Court of Appeals in *Rabidue* ruled that plaintiff's allegations of vulgar and obscene language and displays of posters of nude or partially clad women did not subject her to a hostile, intimidating or offensive work environment. The obscenities, the majority wrote, "although annoying, were not so startling as to have affected seriously the psyches of the plaintiff or other female employees."[5] Further, the poster display had a "*de minimis* effect on the plaintiff's work environment when considered in the context of a society that condones and publicly features and commercially exploits open displays of written and pictorial erotica at the newstands, on prime-time television, at the cinema and in other places."[6]

In a scathing dissent, Judge Keith blasted the majority for not seeing that the "overall circumstances" of plaintiff's workplace evinced an anti-female environment.[7] In his review of the court record, Judge Keith found that a supervisor regularly spewed anti-female obscenities, including referring to women as "whores" "cunt," "pussy," and "tits."[8] Furthermore, female workers were accorded secondary status, repeatedly undermined and not given such job fringe benefits as free lunches, gasoline, telephone credit cards or entertainment privileges that male employees received. In addition, women could not take male customers to lunch, while male employees regularly lunched with female customers. Judge Keith found that supervisors had a "primitive" view of women and an "anti-female animus."[9]

This extremely disparate view of the facts and findings of sexual harassment in *Rabidue* indicates that the majority and dissent operated from different underlying assumptions about sex discrimination. The majority assumed that men and women were equal and used a "reasonable person" standard to decide that women should not have been offended by this workplace environment.[10]

The dissent, on the other hand, utilized a "reasonable woman's" standard because Judge Keith found the reasonable person's perspective "failed to account for the wide divergence between most women's views of appropriate sexual conduct and those of men."[11] He wrote:

> Unless the outlook of the reasonable woman is adopted, the defendants as well as the courts are permitted to sustain ingrained notions of reasonable behaviors fashioned by the offenders, in this case, men.[12]

He continued:

> No woman should be subjected to an environment where her sexual dignity and reasonable sensibilities are visually, verbally or physically, assaulted as a matter of male prerogative.[13]

FOOTNOTES

1 641 F.2d 934, 24 FEP Cases 1155 (D.C. Cir. 1981).

2 454 F.2d 234, 4 FEP Cases 92 (5th Cir. 1971), *cert denied,* 406 U.S. 957, 4 FEP Cases 771 (1972).

3 *Id.* at 238.

4 641 F.2d 934, at 1160.

5 *Rabidue v. Osceola Refining Co.,* 42 FEP Cases 631, at 639.

6 *Id.*

7 *Id.* at 640.

8 *Id.* at 641.

9 *Id.* at 642.

10 *Id.* at 638.

11 *Id.* at 642.

12 *Id.*

13 *Id.* at 643.

§1:08. The Pervasiveness of Sexual Harassment.

What Judge Keith has identified (as described in the previous section) *is* the real danger of a differences approach to sex discrimination in sexual harassment cases. It is not so much that the cause of action will disappear if both males and females are harassed, but that the legal analysis of sexual harassment will fail to see sexual harassment from the perspective of its most likely victim, women. In doing so, such a theory will fail to address the reality of sexual harassment in the workplace. The reality is that sexual harassment is a pervasive practice that is a "standard operating procedure" against women in many workplaces. The courts so characterized the workplace in *Bundy* where the plaintiff was one of the first female employees in the District of Columbia's Department of Corrections and in *Jordan v. Wilson*[1] where the court found that male supervisory officers regularly engaged in the sexual harassment of female officers in the City of Montgomery Police Department.

When the courts fail to see this reality, as the majority did in *Rabidue,* plaintiff attorneys and women's rights advocates criticize the courts for their inability to address the real concerns of women in the workplace. Employers complain that, without a base in reality, court decisions do not consistently guide them as to what is actionable sexual harassment in their workplaces. Finally, no sound legal analysis is being developed to be applied to the next legal question that arises in a sexual harassment case.

This is the legal setting in which this book will explore the current issues in sexual harassment litigation. It is, on one hand, an innovative milieu that has found novel factual allegations of sex harassment to be sex discrimination. On the other hand, it is also an environment confined by basic underlying assumptions about men and women, which, at the very worst, means that sexual harassment is viewed from a male point of view, while women are the majority of its victims.

But it is an exciting legal setting in which to litigate because most of the legal principles of sexual harassment cases are still evolving. The challenge of that evolutionary process is to create sensitive, sound legal doctrine that will effectively address the serious issue of sexual harassment in the workplace.

FOOTNOTES

[1] 42 FEP Cases 950, 965 (D.C. Ala. 1986).

CHAPTER TWO

A Prima Facie Case of Sexual Harassment

§2:01. Overview.

A plaintiff's claim for sexual harassment is derived from Title VII's prohibition that "[i]t shall be an unlawful employment practice for an employer . . . to discriminate against any individual with respect to his . . . terms, conditions or privileges of employment, because of such individual's . . . sex."[1]

Not every instance of sexual harassment gives rise to a federal cause of action. Each claim is scrutinized by the court to see if the plaintiff has set forth certain essential facts which taken together constitute sexual harassment under the statute. These factual elements are proof of a *prima facie* case, the first order of proof in a sex discrimination case.

Once the *prima facie* case is established, then the burden of production shifts to the employer to articulate some legitimate, non-discriminatory reason for the actions it took (e.g. firing the employee, not promoting her), other than sex discrimination. Finally, the plaintiff has an opportunity to prove that the reasons offered by the employer are not the true ones, but merely a pretext for discrimination. The plaintiff retains, however, the ultimate burden of persuading the court by a preponderance of the evidence that she has been the victim of intentional sex discrimination.

This order of proof in disparate treatment cases under Title VII was set forth by the U.S. Supreme Court in *Texas Department of Community Affairs v. Burdine.*[2] Sexual harassment cases have most often been examined under the disparate treatment analysis originated in *McDonnell Douglas Corp. v. Green.*[3] Disparate treatment occurs when members of one sex (e.g. women) are treated differently because of their sex than other persons (e.g. men) who are similarly situated and there is no adequate non-discriminatory reason for that different treatment. These cases ordinarily require proof of intent to discriminate but this has been modified in sexual harassment cases because, as the court explains in *Katz v. Dole,*[4] in the usual case of disparate treatment

> the crux of the matter is the question of motive: was there an intent to discriminate along legally impermissible lines such as race and gender? In cases involving sexual harassment . . . the sexual advance or insult almost always will represent an "intentional assault on an individual's privacy" citing *Bundy,* 641 F.2d at 945.

This book will explore in-depth the three-part order of proof in a disparate treatment Title VII sexual harassment case, beginning in this chapter with the plaintiff's burden to establish a *prima facie* case. The employer's defenses and plaintiff's rebuttal will be addressed in another chapter.

FOOTNOTES

[1] 42 U.S.C. Section 2000e-2(a)(1).

[2] 450 U.S. 248, 252–53, 25 FEP Cases 113 (1981).

[3] 411 U.S. 792, 93 S. Ct. 1817, 36 L.Ed.2d 668, 5 FEP Cases 113 (1981).

[4] 709 F. 2d 251, 31 FEP Cases 1521, 1523–1524 (4th Cir. 1983).

§2:02. Elements of a Prima Facie Case of Sexual Harassment.

In formulating the elements of a *prima facie* case of sexual harassment, courts have relied on the 1980 federal Equal Employment Opportunity Commission's (EEOC) guidelines on sexual harassment. While EEOC guidelines are not binding upon the courts,[1] many courts, including the U.S. Supreme Court in *Meritor Savings Bank v. Vinson,*[2] have deferred to the EEOC guidelines to resolve issues in sexual harassment cases.[3]

The EEOC guidelines define sexual harassment as "unwelcomed sexual advances, requests for sexual favors and other verbal or physical conduct of a sexual nature" when

(1) submission to such conduct is made either explicitly or implicitly a term or condition of an individual's employment,
(2) submission to or rejection of such conduct by an individual is used as the basis for employment decisions affecting such individual, and,
(3) such conduct has the purpose or effect of unreasonably interfering with an individual's work performance or creating an intimidating, hostile or offensive working environment.[4]

From the EEOC guidelines, the courts have identified two forms of sexual harassment.

One is *guid pro quo* sexual harassment, where a supervisor demands sexual favors of a subordinate in exchange for tangible job benefits, such as hiring, promotion, job training or job retention. (e.g. "If you go to bed with me, you'll get a promotion.")

The other form is when the sexual harassment creates a hostile work environment, in which the employee is subjected to verbal conduct (such as sexual innuendo, jokes and sexually derogatory remarks), physical touching or graphic displays of sexually oriented materials. This sexual harassment does not result in a tangible job detriment (e.g. the employee is not fired, demoted or not promoted as a result of the sexual harassment), but the psychological and emotional work environment of the employee is adversely affected. This hostile work environment can be created by a supervisor,[5] or by co-workers,[6] or even a non-employee.[7]

While these two forms of sexual harassment differ, the elements of the *prima facie case* in both are similar. These elements are:

1. The employee is a member of a protected group.

2. The employee has been subjected to "unwelcomed" sexual harassment.
3. The sexual harassment was based on sex.
4. The sexual harassment *or* the employee's response to the sexual harassment affected "terms, conditions or privileges" of employment.
5. The employer was liable for the sexual harassment under *respondeat superior.*

The courts have required different proof for some of the elements of a *prima facie* case for each form of sexual harassment. The proof required in a *quid pro quo* case was first articulated in *Heelan v. Johns-Mansville Corp.*[8] This proof was later refined in *Henson v. City of Dundee.*[9] The elements of a *prima facie* case are also thoroughly discussed in *Katz v. Dole,*[10] and *Jones v. Flagship Intl.*[11]

The proof of a *prima facie* case in a hostile work environment case is derived from *Hanson v. City of Dundee,*[12] and extensively discussed in *Jones v. Flagship Intl.*[13] (In these two cases, the courts dealt with allegations of both *quid pro quo* and hostile work environment sexual harassment.)

Each element of the *prima facie* case will be discussed below, with the variances noted in the proof required for each form of sexual harassment.

FOOTNOTES

[1] *General Electric Co. v. Gilbert,* 429 U.S. 125, 140–45, 97 S. Ct. 401, 410–12, 50 L.Ed.2d 343, 13 FEP Cases 1657 (1976).

[2] —U.S.—, 106 S.Ct. 2399, 2405, 40 FEP Cases 1822 (1986).

[3] *Downes v. F.A.A.,* 775 F.2d 288, 291, 39 FEP Cases 70 (Fed. Cir. 1985); *Henson v. City of Dundee,* 682 F.2d 897, 903, 29 FEP Cases 787 (11th Cir. 1982); *Bundy v. Jackson,* 641 F.2d 934, 947, 24 FEP Cases 1155 (D.C. Cir. 1981); *Walter v. KFGO Radio,* 518 F. Supp. 1309, 1315, 26 FEP Cases 982 (D. N. D. 1981).

[4] 29 C.F.R. Section 1604.11(a).

[5] *Bundy v. Jackson,* 641 F. 2d 934, 124 FEP Cases 1155 (D.C. Cir. 1981); *Rabidue v. Osecola Refining Co.,* 584 F. Supp 419, 36 FEP Cases 183 (E. D. Mich. 1984) *affirmed,* 42 FEP Cases 631, 637 (6th Cir. 1986).

[6] *Zabkowicz v. West Bend Co.*, 589 F. Supp. 780, 35 FEP Cases 611 (D. Wisc. 1974).
[7] *EEOC v. Sage Realty,* 507 F. Supp. 599, 24 FEP Cases 1521 (S.D.N.Y. 1981).
[8] 451 F. Supp. 1382, 20 FEP Cases 251, (D. Col. 1978).
[9] 682 F. 2d. 897, 29 FEP Cases 787 (11th Cir. 1982).
[10] 709 F. 2d 251, 31 FEP Cases 1521 (4th Cir. 1983).
[11] 793 F.2d 714, 43 FEP Cases 358, 362–364 (5th Cir. 1986).
[12] *supra.*
[13] 793 F.2d 714, 43 FEP Cases 358, 365–366 (5th Cir. 1986).

§2:03. —The Employee Is a Member of a Protected Group.

As in other cases of sexual discrimination, this requires a simple stipulation that the employee is a man or a woman.[1]

Women are by far most likely to be victims of sexual harassment. Forty-two percent of women, but only 15 percent of men, reported being sexually harassed over a two-year period in a 1981 study of sexual harassment in the federal workplace by the United States Merit Systems Protection Board (MSPB). In a 1976 survey published by *Redbook* magazine, 88 percent of the more than 9,000 female respondents reported having experienced sexual harassment on the job.

Women are also clearly a protected group under Title VII, although there is scant legislative history on the addition of the word "sex" to Title VII. In *Diaz v. Pan Am. Airways, Inc.*[2] the court has surmised that:

> . . . The amendment adding the word "sex" to "race, color, religion and national origin," was adopted one day before House passage of the Civil Rights Act. It was added on the floor and engendered little relevant debate. In attempting to read Congress' intent in these circumstances, however, it is reasonable to assume, from a reading of the statute itself, that one of Congress' main goals was to provide equal access to the job market for both men and women.

At least one court has ruled that men are likewise protected under Title VII, even though the statutory language itself does not include men unless they are also members of a race, color or national origin group that is covered by Title VII.[3] Protection for men was extended to sexual harassment cases in *Huebschen v. Department of Health and Social Services.*[4] There the court held that a male probationary employee was sexually harassed in violation of Title VII when he was fired by his female supervisor after he terminated a consensual sexual relationship with her. Two courts have found a cause of action when homosexual advances have been alleged. In *Wright v. Methodist Youth Services, Inc.*[5] the courts ruled that a male employee was discriminated against because of his sex when his male supervisor made sexual advances to him that were not directed to women. The court relied on the premise of *Bundy v. Jackson*[6] that ". . . discrimination is *sex* discrimination whenever sex is for no legitimate reason a substantial factor in the discrimination."[7] The *Wright* court also found guidance in *Barnes v. Costle:*[8]

> It is no answer to say that a similar condition could be imposed on a male subordinate by a heterosexual female supervisor, or upon a subordinate of either gender by a homosexual superior of the same gender. In each instance, the legal problem would be identical to that confronting us now—the exaction of a condition which, but for his or her sex, the employee would not have faced.[9]

To date, no reported case of hostile work environment sexual harassment has been brought by a male. A male employee could be subjected to such a sexually charged environment by another man or another woman. Neither case has been seen in the courts.

FOOTNOTES

[1] *Henson, v. City of Dundee, 682 F. 2d 897,* 29 FEP Cases 787, at 792 (11th Cir. 1982).

[2] 442 F. 2d 385, 3 FEP Cases 337, 338 (5th Cir. 1971).

[3] *Local 246, Utility Workers Union of America,* 2 FEP Cases 328 (C.D. Calif. 1969).

See also *Rosen v. Public Service Electric Co.*, 409 F. 2d 775, 1 FEP Cases 708 (3rd. Cir. 1969).

[4] 547 F. Supp. 1168, 32 FEP Cases 1521 (D.C. Wisc. 1982) *reversed on other grounds,* 716 F.2d 1167, 32 FEP Cases 1582 (7th Cir. 1983).

[5] 551 F. Supp. 307, 25 FEP Cases 563 (N.D. Ill. 1981).

[6] 641 F.2d 934, 24 FEP Cases 1155, 1159 (D.C. Cir. 1981).

[7] 551 F. Supp. 307, 25 FEP Cases 563, at 565.
[8] 561 F.2d 985, 990 n. 55, 15 FEP Cases 345, 351 (D.C. Cir. 1977).
[9] Quoted in *Wright,* 551 F. Supp. 307, 25 FEP Cases 563, at 565.
See also *Joyner v. AAA Cooper Transportation*, 597 F. Supp. 537, 36 FEP Cases 1644 (M.D. Ala. 1983).

§2:04. —The Employee Has Been Subjected to "Unwelcome" Sexual Contact.

This element of the *prima facie* case actually examines proof of two elements—the actions alleged are sexual harassment and they are "unwelcomed."

§2:05. ——Quid Pro Quo Sexual Harassment.

In an early reported case of *quid pro quo* sexual harassment[1] the court was concerned that "It is conceivable that under plaintiff's theory flirtation of the smallest order would give rise to liability."[2] The lower court used this as reason to dismiss plaintiff's case for failing to state a cause of action under Title VII but that ruling was overturned on appeal.[3] Later court decisions, while finding sexual harassment actionable under Title VII, continued to question what actions did constitute sexual harassment in the *prima facie* case phase of litigation.

Examples of requests for favors that have been found to constitute sexual harassment are: an invitation to spend the night,[4] an insistence that the employee engage in oral sex,[5] a request to begin a sexual relationship,[6] and a request that employee leave a husband, move into an apartment and have an affair.[7]

But the courts have been clear that a cause of action for sexual harassment does not "arise from an isolated incident or mere flirtation."[8] In early reported cases, the courts did not find *quid pro quo* sexual harassment if the incidents occurred infrequently. The court found no Title VII violation where a male employee in his late seventies once pinched her breast and on another occasion invited her to bed.[9] Also, it was not sexual harassment when one foreman made verbal passes.[10]

Several courts also did not find sexual harassment when the sexual conduct was non-intimidating. That is, when the employee was "not required to endure such treatment in order to keep her job."[11] In *Neeley,* a male vice president told the plaintiff "dirty" jokes and placed his hands on her shoulders while explaining work projects to her, but "none of the acts or statements . . . were related to her continued employment, promotion or compensation by Defendant company."[12] In *Hill v. BASF, Wyandotte Corp.,*[13] the plaintiff failed to establish a *prima facie* case because her supervisor, "never either implicitly or explicitly threatened to put her on probation, terminate her employment or otherwise disadvantage her if she did not consent to his overtures." In *Clark v. World Airways,*[14] the company president made "off-color" remarks, touched her in ways she found offensive and made sexual advances to her but he "never related submission to his advances to any of plaintiff's employment prospects."[15]

FOOTNOTES

[1] *Miller v. Bank of America,* 418 F. Supp. 233, 13 FEP Cases 439 (N.D. Cal. 1976).

[2] *Id.* at 236.

[3] 20 FEP Cases 4362 (9th Cir. 1979).

[4] *Munford v. James T. Barnes & Co.,* 441 F. Supp. 459, 17 FEP Cases 107 (E.D. Mich. 1977).

[5] *Phillips v. Smalley Maint. Services, Inc.,* 711 F.2d 1524, 32 FEP Cases 975 (11th Cir. 1983).

[6] *Barnes v. Costle,* 561 F. 2d 983, 15 FEP Cases 345 (D. C. Cir. 1977).

[7] *Heelan v. Johns-Manville Corp.,* 451 F. Supp. 1382, 20 FEP Cases 251 (D. Colo. 1978).

[8] *Id.* at 1388.

[9] *Pantchenko v. C.B. Dolge,* 18 FEP Cases 689 (D. Conn. 1977) *upheld per curiam* 581 F.2d 1002, 18 FEP Cases 694 (2nd Cir. 1981).

[10] *Smith v. Amoco Chemicals Corp.,* 20 FEP Cases 724 (S.D. Texas 1979).

[11] *Neeley v. American Fidelity Assurance Co.* 17 FEP Cases 482, 485 (W.D. Okla. 1978).

[12] *Id.,* at 485.

[13] 27 FEP Cases 66, 71 (E.D. 1981).

[14] 24 FEP Cases 305 (D.D.C. 1980).

[15] *Id.*

See also *Hall v. F. O. Thacker Co.*, 24 FEP Cases 1499, 1503 (N. D. Georgia 1980); *Robinson v. duPont Co.*, 33 FEP Cases 880, 883 (D. Del. 1979); *Cordes v. County of Yavapai*, 17 FEP Cases 1225, (D.C. Ariz. 1978); *Bundy v. Jackson*, 19 FEP Cases 828, 832 (D.D.C. 1979); *Fisher v. Flynn*, 598 F.2d 663, 19 FEP Cases 932 (1st Cir. 1979); *Vinson v. Taylor*, 23 FEP Cases 37 (D.D.C. 1980).

§2:06. ——Current Standards for Quid Pro Quo Harassment.

These rulings in the *quid pro quo* decisions do not define the standards in *quid pro quo* cases today. For while the *Heelan* court was correct in stating that a cause of action does not arise for isolated incidents of sexual harassment or mere flirtation, the actions in the above cases were decided before the significant 1981 court decision in *Bundy v. Jackson.*[1] In *Bundy,* the appellate court articulated for the first time a cause of action for sexual harassment *absent* a tangible job detriment. (*Hill* was decided after *Bundy* but the ruling in *Bundy* is not discussed there.)

In *Bundy,* the plaintiff alleged that she was subjected to actions (e.g. sexual propositions, advances, and questions about her sexual proclivities) which caused her "emotional harm."[2] But these actions fell short of resulting in an employment consequence to her. There was some evidence however, that a job promotion for the plaintiff was being held up because of her response to the sexual harassment, but this proof was not clear in the record.[3]

The *Bundy* court recognized that if it did *not* find an illegal pattern of harassment here, then "an employer could sexually harass a female employee with impunity by carefully stopping short of firing the employee or taking any other tangible actions against her in response to her resistance."[4] The court added that this leaves the woman three hard choices.

> She can endure the harassment. She can attempt to oppose it, with little hope of success, either legal or practical, but with every prospect of making the job event less tolerable for her. Or she can leave her job, with little hope of legal relief and the likely prospect of another job where she will face harassment anew.[5]

The *Bundy* decision, then, moved the courts beyond the standard *quid pro quo* fact pattern, first identified in *Williams v. Saxbe,*[6] and *Barnes v. Costle,*[7] of a sexual advance, followed by a rejection and then an employment consequence. The appellate court decision in *Bundy* shed new light on the rulings in such cases as *Neeley, Hall, Robinson, Cordes, Fisher* and *Vinson* and *Bundy* in the lower courts, which can be more readily defined as hostile work environment cases rather than *quid pro quo*.

Another *quid pro quo* case of sexual harassment that got reexamined because of *Bundy* was the court's decision in *Corne v. Bausch & Lomb, Inc.*[8] There, the plaintiffs alleged that they were "constructively discharged" when sexual harassment forced them to resign their jobs because of repeated verbal and physical sexual demands by their supervisor which made their work environment intolerable. The court ruled that these sexual demands were merely the "personal proclivity, peculiarity or mannerism" of the male supervisor and nothing in Title VII prohibits verbal and physical advances where the conduct has "no relationship to the nature of the employment."[9]

Catharine MacKinnon in her book, *Sexual Harassment of Working Women,*[10] criticizes the court in *Corne* for not seeing a pattern of sexual harassment and assuming that

> . . . the sexually harassed woman who struggles to endure (the actions of her supervisor) each day because she has (to keep her job in order to) survive (is) said to be having a personal relationship with her harasser? One wonders by what magic a termination can transform a personal relationship into a condition of working—and back again, one presumes, if she is rehired.[11]

MacKinnon found that in *Corne,* the supervisor's actions, limited the plaintiffs to "the choice of putting up with being manhandled or being out of work."[12] She suggests that the courts "define the injury of sexual harassment as the injury of being placed in the position of having to choose between unwanted sex and employment benefits or favorable conditions."[13]

In *Corne* and in court decisions to follow it, the courts have not defined *quid pro quo* sexual harassment in that way yet. But the legal analysis in a hostile work environment sexual harassment case does reflect some of MacKinnon's thinking. That is, under *Bundy,* the injury can be defined at having to choose between unwanted sexual attentions *and* favorable working conditions.

Since *Bundy,* the courts have recognized that a claim for constructive discharge is more viable in a hostile work environment case than in a *quid pro quo* case.[14]

But the courts had found actionable *quid pro quo* cases of sexual harassment before *and* after the court ruling in *Bundy.* The fact patterns that have been found to constitute *quid pro quo* sexual harassment in these cases are:

1. Sexual advances are made by a supervisor and the subordinate is told that if she refuses, she will suffer some job detriment (e.g. she will be fired, demoted, not promoted). She refuses and is fired, demoted or not promoted.[15]
2. An employee declines a sexual advance and she is retaliated against, usually with unjustified criticism of her job performance, harassment, continued harassment and possibly eventual termination.[16] Also included in this category is *Barnes v. Costle.*[17]
3. A potential employee refuses the sexual demands of a senior management official and is refused a job with the company.[18]

Since *Bundy v. Jackson,* the courts have *not* found *quid pro quo* sexual harassment in the following cases:

1) *Bouchet v. National Urban League*[19]—Supervisor was sexually attracted to plaintiff but only "flirted" with her.[20] He made no sexual advances and "did nothing that would amount to sexual harassment."[21]
2) *Sand v. Johnson*[22]—Supervisor only had "moderately flirtatious interest"[23] in plaintiff. There was no "significant longstanding pattern of highly offensive behavior."[24]
3) *Burns v. Terre Haute Regional Hosp.*[25]—Supervisor's sexual conduct (sexual innuendoes, advances) happened long before she was discharged. Incidents were "too attenuated" from date of plaintiff's termination.[26]

4) *Downes v. F.A.A.*[27]—Supervisor's remark asking if plaintiff would ever trade sexual favors to get ahead was not "persistent" and "not used as basis for employment decision."[28]

5) *Jones v. Flagship Int.*[29]—Plaintiff "failed to show that she was required to accept sexual harassment as a condition to the receipt of a job benefit."[30]

FOOTNOTES

[1] 641 F. 2d 934, 24 FEP Cases 1155 (D. C. Cir. 1981).

[2] *Id.* at 1158.

[3] *Id.* at 1157.

[4] *Id.* at 1161.

[5] *Id.* at 1162.

[6] 413 F. Supp. 654, 12 FEP Cases 1093 (D.D.C. 1976).

[7] 561 F.2d 983, 15 FEP Cases 345, (D. C. Cir. 1977).

[8] 390 F. Supp. 161, 10 FEP Cases 289 (D. C. Arizona, 1975).

[9] *Id.* at 163.

[10] MacKinnon, *Sexual Harassment of Working Women*, Yale University Press (1979).

[11] *Id.* at 86.

[12] *Id.* at 61, quoting *Brief for Appellants* at 17.

[13] *Id.*, at 37.

[14] See *Wimberly v. Shoney's Inc.*, 39 FEP Cases 444, 452 (S. D. Geor. 1985); *Robson v. Eva's Supermarket,* 538 F. Supp 857, 30 FEP Cases 1213 (N. D. Ohio, 1982); *Henson v. City of Dundee,* 682 F. Supp. 1309, 29 FEP Cases 787, 796 (11th Cir. 1982) and *Easter v. Jeep Corp.*, 750 F. 2d 520, 42 FEP Cases 666 (6th Cir. 1984). More generally in Title VII cases, see *Young v. Southwestern Savings and Loan Association,* 509 F. 2d 140, 144, 10 FEP Cases 522 (5th Cir. 1975).

[15] *Henson v. City of Dundee,* 682 F. Supp. 1309, 29 FEP Cases 787 (11th Cir. 1982) (Plaintiff refused sexual demands and her request to attend police academy was denied.); *Miller v. Bank of America,* 600 F. 2d 211 20 FEP Cases 462 (9th Cir. 1979), *reversing and remanding,* 418 F. Supp. 233, 13 FEP Cases 439 (N.D. Calif. 1976) (Plaintiff discharged for refusing sexual advances.); *Phillips v. Smalley Maint. Services,* 711 F.2d 1524, 32 FEP Cases 975 (11th Cir. 1983) (Plaintiff fired for refusing sexual advances of owner.); *Ambrose v. U. S. Steel Corp.,* 39 FEP Cases 30 (N. D. Calif. 1985) (Plaintiff's supervisor recommends her discharge after she rejects his sexual demands.); *Craig v. Y & Y Snacks Inc.*, 721 F.2d 77, 33 FEP Cases 187 (3rd Cir. 1983) (Plaintiff discharged after refusing sexual demands of supervisor.); *EEOC v. Domino's Pizzeria, Inc.*, 34 FEP Cases 1075 (E.D. Mich. 1983) (Plaintiff was sexually

assaulted by her supervisor and then discharged after refusing further sexual advances by him.)

[16] See *Garber v. Saxon Business Products,* 552 F. 2d 1032, 15 FEP Cases 344 (4th Cir. 1977); *Stringer v. Commonwealth of Pennsylvania,* 446 F. Supp. 654, 17 FEP Cases 605 (M. D. Pa. 1978); *Heelan v. Johns-Manville Corp.,* 451 F. Supp. 1382, 20 FEP Cases 251 (D. Col. 1978); *Williams v. Saxbe,* 413 F. Supp. 654, 12 FEP Cases 1093 (D.D.C. 1976) *reversed and remanded* (on procedural grounds for a trial *de novo*), *Williams v. Bell, — F.2d. —,* 17 FEP Cases 1664 (D. C. Cir. 1978); *Munford v. James T. Barnes & Co.,* 441 F. Supp. 459, 17 FEP Cases 107 (E.D. Mich. 1977); *Tomkins v. Public Service Electric & Gas,* 568 F. 2d 1044, 16 FEP Cases 22 (3rd Cir. 1977), *reversing and remanding,* 422 F. Supp. 553 (D. N.J. 1976); *Lamb v. Drilco,* 32 FEP Cases 105 (S. D. Tex. 1983); *Mays v. Williamson & Sons Janitorial Services, Inc.,* 591 F. Supp. 1518, 35 FEP Cases 1868 (E. D. Ark. 1984) *affirmed* 39 FEP Cases 106 (8th Cir. 1985); *Meyers v. ITT Diversified Credit Corp.,* 527 F. Supp. 1064, 27 FEP Cases 995 (E. D. Mo. 1981); *Koster v. Chase Manhattan Bank,* 554 F. Supp 285 (S.D.N.Y. 1983).

[17] 561 F. 2d, 983, 15 FEP Cases 345 (D.C. Cir. 1977), *reversing and remanding, Barnes v. Train,* 13 FEP Cases 123 (D.D.C. 1974) (plaintiff refused repeated sexual demands of male supervisor that she engage in social and sexual activities with him, he took away her job duties and eventually abolished her position).

[18] *Rinkel v. Associated Pipeline Contractors,* 17 FEP Cases 224 (D.C. Alaska, 1978).

[19] 33 FEP Cases 536 (D.D.C. 1982).

[20] *Id.* at 540.

[21] *Id.* at 539.

[22] 33 FEP Cases 716 (E. D. Mich. 1982).

[23] *Id.* at 717.

[24] *Id.* at 720.

[25] 581 F. Supp. 1301, 37 FEP Cases 1304 (S.D. Ind. 1983).

[26] *Id.*

[27] 775 F.2d 288, 39 FEP Cases 70 (Fed. Cir. 1985).

[28] *Id.* at 73.

[29] 793 F.2d 714, 41 FEP Cases 358 (5th Cir. 1986).

[30] *Id.* at 364.

§2:07. ——Sexual Favoritism.

The EEOC guidelines and courts have also recognized a cause of action for "sexual favoritism." This occurs when a qualified applicant for a position is rejected in favor of a less qualified applicant because the less qualified applicant has acceded to the sexual demands of the supervisor who made the promotion decision. The EEOC guidelines state this cause of action as:

> Where employment opportunities or benefits are granted because of an individual's submission to the employer's sexual advances or requests for sexual favors, the employer may be held liable for unlawful sex discrimination against other persons who were qualified for but denied that employment opportunity or benefit.[1]

These cases differ from a typical case of a supervisor sexually harassing a subordinate because the plaintiff does not allege that she was the direct target of the sexual harassment. But the courts have ruled that a sexual favoritism case relies on the same theory of sex discrimination as a more typical claim of *quid pro quo* sexual harassment—that "sex [was] for no legitimate reason a substantial factor in the discrimination."[2]

Court decisions in sexual favoritism cases have required, as an additional element of the plaintiff's *prima facie* case, proof of a sexual affair between the two employees.[3]

In *Toscano,* the court found sufficient evidence that the supervisor and the successful applicant for the job promotion were involved in a sexual affair which began prior to the selection of an individual for the promotion.[4]

The supervisor was a self-described "womanizer," the court wrote, who "made no attempt to expunge that aspect of his personality from his work life."[5] He promoted the applicant because he received sexual favors from her and the plaintiff, who was not selected for the promotion, was discriminated against in violation of Title VII.

In *King v. Palmer,* the court decided there was no direct evidence of an explicit sexual relationship between the successful candidate (a nurse) and the supervisor (a doctor). The court wrote, "[both] vigorously deny it existed or even occurred. Dr. Smith has a settled family life with wife and children. Grant (the nurse) has lived an active sex life with other men."[6] The plaintiff argued that even if there was no sexual relationship, Title VII is violated when there is evidence of some kind of sexual attraction, even though unconsummated, between the employees that resulted in the promotion of the successful candidate. The court countered with a question: how could a trier of fact determine, without proof of a sexual relationship, that the selection was made for reasons of sexual attractiveness as opposed to "an individual's nonsexual traits and qualities of personality?"[7] Thus, the court concluded,

> Cases in this category must not rest on rumor, knowing winks and purient overtones or on inferences allowed in divorce law. Plaintiff offered no positive proof of sexual conduct or sexual attractiveness as between (the nurse) and the doctor who promoted her. She has therefore failed to meet her burden.[8]

While the existence of direct proof of a sexual relationship was pivotal to the district court decisions in these two cases, the proof in *Toscano* was most egregious. The supervisor telephoned the plaintiff at home and "sang love songs in Spanish."[9] He called the plaintiff and other female employees at home and at work to proposition them and brag about his sexual prowess. The employer was not without notice of this behavior but did nothing to stop it and, in fact, it promoted the supervisor.[10]

A more likely situation is closer to the facts in *King*, where female employees could have easily perceived that there were sexual favors to be traded in order to gain job benefits. Whether Title VII's prohibitions will be interpreted to extend to those instances is yet to be determined by a higher court.[11]

Footnotes

[1] 29 C.F.R. Section 1604 (g).

[2] *King v. Palmer,* 778 F.2d 878, 35 FEP Cases 1302 (D.D.C. 1984), quoting *Bundy v. Jackson,* 641 F.2d 934, 942–43, 24 FEP Cases 1155 (D.C. Cir. 1981).

[3] *King v. Palmer,* 778 F.2d 878, 35 FEP Cases 1302 (D.D.C. 1984); *Toscano v. Nimmo,* 570 F. Supp. 1197, 32 FEP Cases 1401 (D. Del. 1983).

[4] 570 F. Supp. 1197, 32 FEP Cases 1401, at 1404.

[5] *Id.*

[6] 778 F.2d 878, 35 FEP Cases 1302, at 1304.

[7] *Id.*

[8] *Id.*

[9] 570 F. Supp. 1197, 32 FEP Cases 1401, at 1403.

[10] *Id.* at 1407.

[11] See *Simmons v. Lyons,* 746 F.2d 265, 36 FEP Cases 411 (5th Cir. 1984) where the appellate court found that the plaintiff had raised a genuine issue of fact as to whether she and her mother had not been rehired because the daughter had rejected the sexual advances of the sheriff.

§2.08. ——Hostile Environment Cases.

Bundy v. Jackson[1] was a benchmark decision because the federal appellate court clearly articulated a cause of action for hostile work environment cases under Title VII. *Brown v. City of Guthrie,*[2] decided eight months before *Bundy* also established a hostile work environment cause of action. Two months later, the Minnesota Supreme Court made a similar analysis in *Continental Can Co. v. State of Minnesota.*[3]

In *Bundy,* the court adopted the reasoning of Judge Goldberg in *Rogers v. EEOC,*[4] a race discrimination case where the work environment was "so heavily polluted with discrimination as to destroy completely the emotional and psychological stability of minority group workers."[5] The *Bundy* court found that "the sexually stereotyped insults and demeaning stereotyped insults and demeaning propositions to which she (the plaintiff) was indisputably subjected and which caused her anxiety and debilitation, illegally poisoned that environment."[6]

The court added:

> Racial slurs, though intentional and directed at individuals, may still be just verbal insults, yet they too may create Title VII liability. How then can sexual harassment, which injects the most demeaning sexual stereotypes into the general work environment and which always represents an intentional assault on an individual's innermost privacy, not be illegal.[7]

Following *Bundy,* the court in *Henson v. City of Dundee,*[8] observed:

> Sexual harassment which creates a hostile or offensive environment for members of one sex is every bit the arbitrary barrier to sexual equality at the workplace that racial harassment is to racial equality. Surely, a requirement that a man or woman run a gauntlet of sexual abuse in return for the privilege of being allowed to work and make a living can be as demeaning and disconcerting as the harshest of racial epithets.

Since *Bundy,* courts have uniformly upheld a cause of action under Title VII for hostile work environment sexual harassment, including the U. S. Supreme Court in *Meritor Savings Bank v. Vinson.*[9]

The question explored in the subsequent cases, however, is what kind of actions must be alleged and proven in a hostile work environment sexual harassment case. In *Henson,* the court, drew from the language of the EEOC guidelines, that the sexual harassment must create "an intimidating, hostile or offensive working environment."[10] The court held that the sexual harassment

> . . . must be sufficiently pervasive so as to alter the conditions of employment and create an abusive working environment. Whether sexual harassment at the workplace is sufficiently severe and persistent to affect seriously the psychological well being of employees is a question to be determined with regard to the totality of the circumstances.[11]

In *Katz v. Dole,*[12] the court looked for and found a "pattern of personally directed sexual insult and innuendo" present in the FAA workplace, where plaintiff was the only woman air traffic controller.[13]

> This harassment took the form of extremely vulgar and offensive sexually related epithets addressed to and employed about Katz by supervisory personnel as well as other controllers. The words used were ones widely recognized as not only improper but as intensely degrading, deriving their power to wound not only from their meaning but also from "the disgust and violence they express phonetically."[14]

The U. S. Supreme Court in *Meritor Savings Bank*[15] affirmed the *Henson* criteria and noted in *Meritor Savings Bank,* that the sexual harassment alleged was not only "pervasive but also criminal conduct of the most serious nature" and "plainly sufficient to state a claim for hostile environment sexual harassment."[16] There, the plaintiff proved, at trial, that her supervisor made "repeated demands for sexual favors, fondled her in front of other employees, followed her into the women's restroom when she went there alone, exposed himself to her and even forcibly raped her on several occasions." These activities ceased when the plaintiff started going with a steady boyfriend.[17]

Since the *Bundy* decision in 1981, the courts have found the following situations to be sexual harassment that created a "intimidating, hostile or offensive working environment":

1) *Morgan v. Hertz Corp.,*[18]—Suggestive indecent comments and direct questions of a sexual nature were part of "history of vulgar and indecent language tolerated by management and directed at women. The proof is clear that the order of the day at Hertz is for supervisory men to address questions about sexual activity and preference to women rental representatives."[19]

2) *Henson v. City of Dundee,*[20]—Police chief subjected two women to "numerous harangues of demeaning sexual inquiries and vulgarities" over a two-year period.[21] In addition, he "repeatedly requested that she have sexual relations with him."

3) *Coley v. Conrail,*[22]—Supervisor "consistently made sexually explicit and demeaning remarks," which included references to the size of her "boobs," keeping track of her menstrual periods on his office calendar and making remarks about her moods in relation thereto, and repeated inquiries as to when she was going to "do something nice for him."[23] The court found this to be "sufficiently severe and persistent."[24]

4) *Robson v. Eva's Supermarket,*[25]—Co-worker, who also acted as plaintiff's supervisor, offered her $100 to go to bed with him. He asked her to wear "tight jeans" to work so he could watch her walk by. He continuously made profane and sexually suggestive comments to her and stared or leered at her body.

Once he felt the back of her blouse without her permission to see if she was wearing a bra. He patted her on the buttocks and twice physically assaulted her, once by grabbing her arm and another time by pulling her face toward his.[26] The court found the conduct to have created an "intimidating, hostile and offensive" work environment.[27]

5) *Martin v. Norbar, Inc.*[28]—Co-worker told lewd stories, asked her to go to bed, touched her legs and thighs several times.[29] The court denied employer's motion for summary judgment.

6) *Zabkowicz v. West Bend Co.,*[30]—Plaintiff, only one of two women warehouse workers, was harassed by male co-workers. They made comments about whether she was wearing a bra, referred to her as "sexy bitch," "hot and horny," "slut" and "cunt," and posted, over a three-year period, approximately 75 sexually oriented drawings in the warehouse which referred to plaintiff in derogatory terms. Within a two-year period, one co-worker exposed his buttocks to her between 10–20 times. The court held that this "sustained, malicious and brutal harassment" was "more than merely unreasonable; it was malevolent and outrageous."[31]

7) *Jeppsen v. Wunnicke.*[32]

8) *Katz v. Dole,*[33]—Plaintiff was subjected to "a pattern of personally directed sexual insult and innuendo"[34] which was not "isolated or trivial."[35]

9) *Vinson v. Taylor,*[36]—Plaintiff's supervisor made "repeated demands for sexual favors, fondled her in front of other employees, followed her into the women's restroom when she went there alone, exposed himself to her and even forcibly raped her on several occasions." These activities ceased when the plaintiff started going with a steady boyfriend.[37] The court remanded the case to the district court which had "fatally undermined the legal conclusion that Vinson did not suffer a violation of Title VII."[38]

10) *Ambrose v. U.S. Steel Corp.*[39]—Plaintiff's supervisor was "flirtatous" with her, asked plaintiff about her dating habits, asked her views on oral sex, said he thought she would be "good in bed," and made sexual advances toward her.[40] The court found "not only was she subject to his frequent unwanted sexual advances, but also she was forced to tolerate his persistent, probing questions of her personal life."[41] The court concluded: "There is no doubt that a discriminatory work environment existed at U.S. Steel."[42]

11) *Delgado v. Lehman,*[43]—Plaintiff was sexually harassed by actions of head of equal employment opportunity office, including "abusive" comments, "unprofessional" treatment of women employees and "stuffing" piece of paper down plaintiff's blouse.[44] These were not "isolated or genuinely trivial" actions.[45]

Footnotes

[1] 641 F. 2d 934, 24 FEP Cases 1155 (D. C. Cir. 1981)

[2] 22 FEP Cases 1627 (W.D. Oklahoma 1980).

[3] 22 FEP Cases 1808 (Minn. 1980).

[4] 454 F. 2d 234, 4 FEP Cases 92 (5th Cir. 1971) *cert. denied,* 406 U. S. 957, 4 FEP Cases 771 (1972).

[5] *Id.* 454 F. 2d at 238, 4 FEP Cases at 94.

[6] 641 F. 2d 934, 24 FEP Cases 1155, at 1160.

[7] *Id.* at 1161.

[8] 682 F.2d 897, 29 FEP Cases 787, 791 (11th Cir. 1982).

[9] —U.S.—, 106 S. Ct. 2399, 2405, 40 FEP Cases 1822, 54 LW 4703 (1986).

[10] 29 C.F.R. Section 1604.11(a) (29 FEP Cases at 792).

[11] 682 F. 2d 897, 29 FEP Cases 787, at 794.

[12] 709 F. 2d 251, 31 FEP Cases 1521 (4th Cir. 1983).

[13] *Id.* at 1523.

[14] Quoting C. Miller and K. Swift, *Words and Women* 109 (1977). *Id.* at 1522.

[15] 106 Sup. Ct. 2399, at 2406.

[16] *Id.*

[17] *Id.* at 2402.

[18] 542 F. Supp. 123, 27 FEP Cases 990 (W. D. Tenn, 1981).

[19] *Id.* at 994.

[20] 682 F.2d 897, 29 FEP Cases 787 (11th Cir. 1982).

[21] *Id.* at 789.
[22] 561 F. Supp. 645, 34 FEP Cases 129 (E. D. Mich. 1982).
[23] *Id.* at 131.
[24] *Id.* at 133.
[25] 538 F. Supp. 857, 30 FEP Cases 1213 (N.D. Ohio 1982).
[26] *Id.* at 1214.
[27] *Id.* at 1215.
[28] 537 F. Supp. 1260, 30 FEP Cases 103 (S. D. Ohio 1982).
[29] *Id.*
[30] 589 F. Supp. 780, 35 FEP Cases 610 (E. D. Wisc. 1984).
[31] *Id.* at 613.
[32] 611 F. Supp. 78, 37 FEP Cases 994 (D. Alaska 1985).
[33] 709 F.2d 251, 31 FEP Cases 1521 (4th Cir. 1983).
[34] *Id.* at 1523.
[35] *Id.* at 1524.
[36] 753 F.2d 141, 36 FEP Cases 1423 (D.C. Cir. 1985).
[37] 106 S. Ct. 2399, at 2402.
[38] *Id.* at 1426.
[39] 39 FEP Cases 30 (D. Calif. 1985).
[40] *Id.* at 34.
[41] *Id.*
[42] *Id.* at 34–35.
[43] 43 FEP Cases 593 (E.D. Va. 1987).
[44] *Id.* at 599.
[45] *Id.*

§2:09. ——Insufficient Illegal Conduct Under Title VII.

In the following cases since the 1981 *Bundy* decision, the courts have *not* found the sexual harassment to be sufficiently severe or pervasive to constitute illegal conduct under Title VII.

1) *Walter v. KFGO Radio*[1]—Plaintiff's supervisor "patted on her bottom" three to five times, touched her "breast area" and made inebriated attempts at getting her to have an affair with him. The court found this behavior "insufficient" to constitute sexual harassment.[2]

2) *Hayden v. Cox Enterprises*[3]—Plaintiff, a journeyman printer, was "bumped" twice by her co-workers. The court finds these acts "fall far short of egregious."[4]

3) *Ukarish v. Magnesium Elecktron*[5]—Plaintiff, only female production worker, "joined in . . . as one of the boys" in "sexual banter" and "sexual language" in workplace. This atmosphere was "continuing," "pervasive" and "distasteful"[6] but did not have "a serious and significant impact" on plaintiff in her job.[7]

4) *Downes v. F.A.A.*[8]—Plaintiff's allegations of five instances of sexual harassment in a three-year period do not establish a "pattern of harassment directed to female employees or to a particular employee . . . (or) repeated to the point where it is 'routine' or 'of a generalized nature . . .' "[9] Supervisors's acts included referring to plaintiff as "the Dolly Parton of the office," speculating in a telephone conversation with her on the frequency of plaintiff's sexual relationships after her divorce, describing a female non-employee who wore tight shorts and repeating a crude "Bob Hope joke" about such attire to the staff and touching plaintiff's hair on two occasions.[10]

5) *Ferguson v. duPont*[11]—Plaintiff was subjected to sexual comments and remarks and she was touched physically once. The court ruled this was not "pervasive."[12]

6) *Scott v. Sears Roebuck and Co.*[13]—Plaintiff claimed she was made "uncomfortable" by repeated sexual propositions, winks, suggestion that co-worker "rub down" her body, was slapped on her buttocks and asked for sexual favors. Court found acts were not repeated and relentless and were "subtle behaviors" and comments that "were susceptible of innocent intent."[14]

7) *Wimberly v. Shoney's Inc.*[15]—Plaintiffs' allegations of acts of physical touching, indecent propositions, obscene and lewd comments and use of profanity were not found to be "continuous, sustained and pervasive sexually-oriented misconduct. In total, they were random, sometimes meaningless encounters."[16]

8) *Rabidue v. Osceola Refining Co.*[17]—Plaintiff alleged co-worker's display of partially clad or nude posters of women and

supervisor's "crude, vulgar language" created hostile, offensive intimidating work environment. The lower court found that "language was annoying but not so shocking or severe," and "posters were not so drastic."[18]

9) *Freedman v. American Standard*[19]—Plaintiff received "obscene message" from company employee, sexual advances from co-worker. Not sufficient to constitute sexual harassment.[20]

10) *Evans v. Mail Handlers Union*[21]—Plaintiff had "consensual" sexual relationship with supervisor. She did not consider work environment with this supervisor "intimidating" or "offensive" until relationship deteriorated. Here, environment was "substantially welcomed" by plaintiff.[22]

11) *Loftin-Boggs v. City of Meridian*[23]—Plaintiff failed to prove "crude language and storytelling" was offensive when she participated in and even initiated it.[24]

12) *Vermett v. Hough*[25]—Plaintiff, a state police trooper, failed to show one act of co-worker shining a flashlight through her legs and moving it up her body was sexual harassment. The court found this was not an act of a sexual nature—"Childish, yes, sexual harassment, no."[26]

13) *Jones v. Flagship Int.*[27]—Plaintiff's allegation of only three sex-related incidents does not establish case of illegal sexual harassment. The court found this "not sufficiently pervasive."[28]

14) *Neville v. Taft Broadcasting Co.*[29]—Plaintiff was once "grabbed and kissed against her will" by her supervisor and subject to his "occasional unwelcomed physical contact of a non-sexual nature."[30] The court found this "insufficient to constitute" sexual harassment.[31]

15) *Sardigal v. St. Louis National Stockyards Co.*[32]—Plaintiff, a waitress, alleged incidents of sexual advances, remarks and

other offensive or abusive actions. Some the court found she did not prove, others were not unwelcomed.[33] The court found this "insufficient to constitute" sexual harassment.[34]

16) *Highlander v. KFC National Management Co.*[35]—Plaintiff did not prove her claim where she initiated contact with supervisor in bar that led to acts of sexual harassment.

17) *Sapp v. City of Warner-Robins*[36]—Plaintiff alleged one incident of sexual harassment. The court found "single effort (by supervisor) to get plaintiff to go out with him was not of a repeated or continuous nature to be sufficiently pervasive enough to affect plaintiff's psychological well being."[37]

18) *Selligson v. MIT*[38]—Plaintiff alleged that supervisor asked her "personal" questions. The court found that male employees were likewise monitored and acts were not "sufficiently severe" to constitute harassment.[39]

19) *Williams-Hill v. Donovan*[40]—Plaintiff was subjected to sexist and ethnic jokes that were offensive but this atmosphere did not constitute violation of Title VII.[41]

From these cases, some patterns do emerge. The courts have examined the allegations of sexual misconduct under a standard that the actions must be sufficiently "pervasive" "severe and persistent" and show a "pattern" of actions "personally directed" at the plaintiff. Some courts have found the sexual harassment when the actions were "more than merely unreasonable" and "malevolent and outrageous."[42] The U. S. Supreme Court in *Meritor Savings Bank,* noted that criminal conduct of the most severe nature" (e.g. rape) was sexual harassment.[43] However, the fact patterns are not always consistent. In some cases the courts have found obscene language to be sexual harassment (*Morgan, Zabkowicz*); in other cases, it has not been (*Rabidue*). Physical touching has sometimes been actionable (*Robson, Martin*), other times not (*Wimberly, Walter, Ferguson, Scott,* and *Neville*).

Two things are clear. One, as the court notes in *Downes v. FAA,*[44] whether an action is sexual harassment will be judged by "the totality of the circumstances," a standard also set forth in the EEOC guidelines on sexual harassment.[45]

Second, while there are some inconsistent holdings in specific cases of sexual harassment, the range of the kinds of actions found to be sexual harassment is quite broad. It includes verbal conduct, sexual advances, sexual innuendo, profane or obscene language and displays of sexually oriented materials. This broad range of actions will be examined under a consistent standard which has been endorsed by the U.S. Supreme Court in *Meritor Savings Bank v. Vinson*. What remains is for the jurisprudence in the sexual harassment area to continue to evolve.

FOOTNOTES

1 518 F. Supp 1309, 26 FEP Cases 982 (D. N.D. 1981).
2 *Id.* at 986.
3 534 F. Supp. 1166, 28 FEP Cases 1315 (N. D. Geo. 1982).
4 *Id.* at 1325.
5 31 FEP Cases 1315 (D. N. J. 1983).
6 *Id.* at 1319.
7 *Id.* at 1321.
8 775 F.2d 288, 39 FEP 70 (Fed. Cir. 1985).
9 *Id.* at 75.
10 *Id.* at 74.
11 560 F. Supp. 1172, 31 FEP Cases 795 (D. Del. 1983).
12 *Id.* at 813.
13 605 F. Supp. 1047, 37 FEP Cases 878 (N. D. Ill 1985), *affirmed,* 798 F.2d 210, 41 FEP Cases 805 (7th Cir. 1986).
14 *Id.* 37 FEP at 883.
15 39 FEP Cases 444 (S. D. Geo. 1985).
16 *Id.* at 453.
17 584 F. Supp. 419, 36 FEP Cases 183 (E. D. Mich. 1984), *affirmed* 42 FEP Cases 631 (6th Cir. 1986).
18 *Id.* at 193.
19 41 FEP Cases 471 (D. N.J. 1986).
20 *Id.* at 476.
21 711 F.2d 1524, 32 FEP Cases 634 (D.D.C. 1983).
22 *Id.* at 637.
23 633 F. Supp. 532 (S.D. Miss. 1986).
24 *Id.*
25 627 F. Supp. 587, 42 FEP Cases 1432 (W. D. Mich. 1986).

[26] *Id.* at 1448.
[27] 793 F.2d 714, 41 FEP Cases 358 (5th Cir. 1986).
[28] *Id.* at 363.
[29] 42 FEP Cases 1314 (W.D.N.Y. 1987).
[30] *Id.* at 1316–17.
[31] *Id.* at 1317.
[32] 42 FEP Cases 447 (S.D. Ill. 1986).
[33] *Id.* at 502.
[34] *Id.*
[35] 805 F.2d 644, 42 FEP Cases 654 (6th Cir. 1986).
[36] 43 FEP Cases 486 (N.D. Georgia 1987).
[37] *Id.* at 491.
[38] 43 FEP Cases 823 (D. Mass. 1987).
[39] *Id.* at 829.
[40] 43 FEP Cases 253 (M.D. Fla. 1987).
[41] *Id.* at 258.
[42] 589 F. Supp. 780, 35 FEP Cases 610, at 613.
[43] 106 Sup. Ct. 2399, at 2406.
[44] 775 F.2d 897, 39 FEP Cases 70 (Fed. Cir. 1980).
[45] 29 C.F.R. Section 1604.11(b).

§2:10. ——Proof of Unwelcome Sexual Contact.

A second inquiry on this element of the *prima facie* case is what proof is needed that the sexual contact is "unwelcome"?

Before examining court cases on this issue, it must be acknowledged that what is unwelcomed or unwanted by one individual may not be so for another. Psychiatrist Carroll Brodsky has found that sexual "teasing" can be benign and mutually pleasurable in the workplace.

> Healthy teasing is a part of a sociocultural ritual for approaching a topic such as sex respectfully.[1]

But, she adds, if one of the parties lacks the requisite sensitivity or skill, the teasing may escalate into harassment.

> In contrast to teasing, harassment is not mutually satisfactory and is not enjoyable to all persons engaged in it. Harassment is an interaction in which one person purposefully seeks to discomfort the other person.[2]

A lack of reciprocal feelings on the part of one employee escalates a sexual advance into sexual harassment, Brodsky says. This is consistent with research data that suggests that men often misread a women's feelings about sexual attentions on the job. While it is assumed by men that women welcome their attentions, only 15 percent of the 9,000 respondents in a 1976 *Redbook* magazine survey[3] described it as "flattering" to be the object of the sexual advances, sexual attentions or visual leering or ogling they had received in the workplace.[4] Seventy-five percent of the women surveyed found these unwelcomed attentions "embarrassing," "demeaning" and "insulting."[5] Furthermore, 92 percent of the respondents said that this situation was a problem, a majority describing it as a "serious one," since it "undermines a woman's job performance causing her emotional and physical suffering."[6]

In addition, men and women see sexual harassment differently. In the MSPB study of the federal workplace, male and female participants were asked to identify which of the following behaviors they thought were sexual harassment.

1. Uninvited pressure for sexual favors,
2. Uninvited and deliberate touching, leaning over, cornering or pinching,
3. Uninvited sexually suggestive looks or gestures,
4. Uninvited letters, phone calls or materials of a sexual nature,
5. Uninvited pressure for dates, and,
6. Uninvited sexual teasing, jokes, remarks or questions.

A majority of the female participants in the study identified all six of these behaviors as sexual harassment whether initiated by supervisors or co-workers. Male participants, on the other hand, only found all six to be sexual harassment if done by supervisors, not co-workers. They did not consider sexually suggestive looks, gestures, remarks, joking or teasing to be harassment when done by co-workers.

But in order to look at what is unwelcomed, it is also important to examine why women do acquiesce to sexual advances at work. Many fear economic sanctions, i.e. loss of a promotion, salary increases or their job. The court in *Jeppsen v. Wunnicke,*[7] recognized this fact.

> The practical problem is that the employee who stays on the job the longest and puts up with the most offensive sexual harassment is more likely than not going to be the employee who is most dependent on retaining the job. Worst yet, this same employee is likely to be the one most reticient to complain . . . lest . . . her complaint was not taken seriously, poor performance ratings started appearing, and ultimately, a promotion was denied.[8]

In *Ambrose v. U.S. Steel Corp.,*[9] the court noted that the plaintiff was divorced with four children, had house payments and an alcoholic ex-husband. "She could not risk losing her job."[10]

The MSPB study of the federal workplace also indicated that nearly seven out of every ten female victims of sexual harassment said that at the time they experienced the harassment, they needed their jobs a great deal.[11]

The court in *Horn v. Duke Homes*[12] recognized that a harasser may in fact prey on female employees who are most vulnerable. There, several female employees (beside the plaintiff) testified that the supervisor had the "propensity to use his powers at Duke to sexually exploit women who were vulnerable because of marital problems and financial dependency on their jobs."[13] Several women approached by this male supervisor for sexual favors were either divorced or separated from their husbands at the time.[14]

In Title VII litigation, what the courts have focused on however, is the tangible ways in which a plaintiff has indicated that the conduct is "unwelcome."

Footnotes

[1] From "Rape at Work," at 49 in Walker, *Sexual Assault,* Lexington Books, 1976.

[2] *Id.* at 50.

[3] "What Men Do to Women on the Job: A Shocking Look at Sexual Harassment," by Claire Safran, *Redbook,* November, 1976.

[4] *Id.* at 217.

[5] *Id.* at 217.

[6] *Id.* at 149, 217.
[7] 611 F. Supp. 78, 37 FEP Cases 994 (D.C. Alaska, 1985).
[8] *Id.* at 997.
[9] 39 FEP Cases 30 (D. Calif. 1985).
[10] *Id.* at 32.
[11] MSPB at 46.
[12] 755 F.2d 599, 37 FEP Cases 229 (7th Cir. 1985).
[13] *Id.* at 230.
[14] *Id.*

§2:11. ——Proof of Unwelcome Sexual Contact In a Quid Pro Quo Case.

In a *quid pro quo* sexual harassment case, that a sexual advance is unwelcome can obviously be indicated by a rejection of the sexual demands. But, while the courts have accepted a fact pattern in *quid pro quo* cases that Catherine MacKinnon labels in her book, "the triology of unwanted advances, rejection and retaliation,"[1] proof of rejection is sometimes difficult. It may be hard even to show that the sexual advances occurred, let alone that they were rejected. This requires a difficult credibility determination by the court as to which party is telling the truth, especially when the alleged harasser categorically denies every allegation of sexual harassment or the court may find that there are no eyewitnesses to the events that supposedly transpired between the parties.[2]

Other indication of "unwelcome" sexual conduct in a *quid pro quo* case is that the sexual demands are repeatedly rejected. In *Heelan v. Johns-Mansville Corp.*[3] the court found unwelcomed sexual advances where a plaintiff had been sexually harassed by her supervisor for two years. That was, the court wrote, the "paradigm of the repreated, unwelcomed sexual advance."[4]

Footnotes

[1] Mackinnon, *Sexual Harassment of Working Women*, Yale University Press (1979), at 33.

[2] See *Munford v. James T. Barnes & Co.*, 441 F. Supp. 459, 17 FEP Cases 107 (E.D. Mich. 1977); *Horn v. Duke Homes*, 775 F.2d 599, 37 FEP Cases 228 (7th Cir. 1985); *Craig v. Y & Y Snacks Inc.*, 721 F.2d 77, 33 FEP Cases 187 (3rd Cir. 1983); *Mays v. Williamson & Sons Janitorial Services, Inc.*, 591 F. Supp. 1518,

35 FEP Cases 1868 (E. D. Ark. 1984) *affirmed,* 775 F.2d 258, 39 FEP Cases (8th Cir. 1985). See also the discussion on credibility and corroboration of evidence in a later chapter of this book.

[3] 451 F. Supp. 1382, 20 FEP Cases 1382 (D. Col. 1978).

[4] *Id.* at 1389.

§2:12. ——Proof of Unwelcome Sexual Contact in Hostile Environment Cases.

In a hostile work environment case, the court in *Henson v. City of Dundee,*[1] determined whether the conduct was unwelcomed by "the sense that the employee did not solicit or incite it and in the sense that the employee regarded the conduct as undesirable or offensive."[2] This concept was derived from the court's decision in *Gan v. Kepro Circuit Systems.*[3] In *Gan,* the plaintiff

> "regularly used crude and vulgar language and initiated sexually-oriented conversations with her male and female co-workers. She frequently asked male employees about their marital sex lives and whether they engaged in extra-marital sexual relationships. Plaintiff also made her own marital sexual relationships a regular topic of office conversation.[4]

The *Gan* court, concluding that the alleged harassment was "substantially welcomed and encouraged by the plaintiff," held that no sexual harassment had occurred.[5]

However, frequently "coarse and crude" language in a workplace can mistakenly be perceived as welcome by an employee. This is particularly assumed about women in non-traditional jobs, as in *Halpert v. Wertheim & Co.,*[6] where the plaintiff, a trader of securities in a brokerage firm, claimed she was sexually harassed by the conduct of other traders on the firm's institutional trading desk. But the court denied her claim because this use of language was "known" to the plaintiff and "condoned."

> The language of this marketplace was coarse, and frequent references were made to male and female genitalia and to sexual activity. This language was referred to at the trial as "truck driver" language, though such references have been heard in other occupations, includ-

> ing even the most reflective. (Plaintiff) was the subject of such language on occasion as were other women with whom the traders had contact. (She) on occasion used such language with reference to her own activities and those of others.[7]

In *Ukarish v. Magnesium Elektron*[8] the court likewise found in rejecting her claim of sexual harassment that the plaintiff appeared to accept and to join in as "one of the boys" in the language of this workplace, here a chemical production plant. The court wrote:

> However distasteful this language might be in a court of law, it was nevertheless the rather customary plant language that pervaded that atmosphere. It was no better or no worse than it had been before (the plaintiff) arrived and was not directed at her either by . . . (her co-)workers on the job in any intensified degree.[9]

The court in *Morgan v. Hertz Corp.,*[10] realized that it was "the order of the day" for supervisory male employees to ask questions about sexual activity and preferences to women in the Hertz workplace. Yet the court found, while some women did not mind and even participated in the comments and remarks, that "the plaintiff did not appreciate the remarks and that many of the other women did not either."[11] For this reason, the court concluded that the plaintiff had proven her claim.

FOOTNOTES

[1] 682 F.2d 897, 29 FEP Cases 787 (11th Cir. 1982).

[2] *Id.* at 792.

[3] 28 FEP Cases 637 (E. D. Mo. 1982).

[4] *Id.* at 640.

[5] *Id.* at 641.

See also *Highlander v. KFC National Management Co.,* 805 F.2d 644, 42 FEP Cases 654 (6th Cir. 1986) (where plaintiff did not prove her claim since she had initiated meeting with supervisor in bar that led to acts of sexual harassment); *Loftin-Boggs v. City of Meridian,* 633 F. Supp 1323, 41 FEP Cases 532 (S.D. Miss. 1986), (where plaintiff "participated in and even initiated" some of the crude language and storytelling and failed to tell any supervisors or fellow workers that she found the environment unwelcome, the court found no violation of Title VII).

[6] 27 FEP Cases 21 (S. D. N. Y. 1980).

[7] *Id.* at 23–24.

[8] 31 FEP Cases 1315 (D. N. J. 1983).

[9] *Id.* at 1319.

See also *Vermett v. Hough*, 627 F. Supp. 587, 42 FEP Cases 1432 (W. D. Mich. 1986) (where there was "ample evidence" that plaintiff engaged in horseplay and joking with male state police troopers and used vulgar language occasionally as a way to be accepted by the men, so that the court ruled that the plaintiff did not prove a violation of Title VII).

[10] 542 F. Supp. 123, 27 FEP Cases 990 (W. D. Tennessee 1981).

[11] *Id.* at 994.

§2:13. ——Proof of Unwelcome Sexual Contact When Plaintiff and Defendant Had a Prior Consensual Sexual Relationship.

Several courts have also held sexual conduct not to be unwelcomed when, as in *Evans v. Mailhandlers,*[1] the plaintiff and defendant supervisor had a previous consensual sexual relationship. The court, noting that the plaintiff did not consider the conduct of her supervisor to be offensive or intimidating until the relationship deteriorated, ruled that the "allegedly harassing conduct was substantially welcomed" by the plaintiff. Her claim for sexual harassment failed, the court concluded, even though evidence at trial had established a workplace environment that was "very distasteful."[2]

However, in *Meritor Savings Bank v. Vinson,*[3] the U. S. Supreme Court cautioned in a case where the plaintiff had engaged in prior consensual sexual relations with her supervisor, that "(t)he correct inquiry is whether the respondent by her conduct indicated that the alleged sexual advances were unwelcome."[4] Thus, the Court did not preclude a case in whih the "voluntary" submission to sexual conduct could still be "unwelcome."

Footnotes

[1] 32 FEP Cases 634 (D.D.C. 1983).

[2] *Id.* at 637.

[3] —U.S.—, 106 S.Ct. 2399, 40 FEP Cases 1822, 54 LW 4703 (1986).

[4] *Id.* at 4707.

§2:14. ——The Perspective for Assessing if Sexual Conduct Is Unwelcome.

Finally, the courts have considered what perspective is to be used in judging if the sexual conduct is unwelcome. That is, is sexual harassment to be viewed through the eyes of the individual who is being harassed (a subjective standard) or should the court set an objective standard of how a "reasonable person" in the same situation would have seen the conduct?

In *Sand v. Johnson*[1] the court found Sand, the plaintiff, "hypersensitive to conduct by men."[2] The court asked "whether it should be a subjective or objective standard applied to conduct Sand may have perceived as sexual and a work environment she may have perceived as intimidating, hostile and offensive."[3] In the end, the court applied an objective standard and took into account the perceptions of the plaintiff's male co-workers. The court observed:

> At the Company, (the plaintiff) . . . worked in a male dominated environment. During the course of (her) . . . employment the other designers saw nothing unusual in (the supervisor's) . . . conduct toward Sand and his conversations with her. Sand, however, gave (his) conduct and conversations a sexual connotation.[4]

Thus, with this objective standard, the court discredited the plaintiff's testimony about these events, and finding no one to corroborate her testimony, denied her claim.[5]

The EEOC guidelines take another view. The guidelines state that unwelcome sexual behavior which "has the *effect* of unreasonably interfering with an individual's work performance or creating an intimidating, hostile or offensive work environment" is sexual harassment.[6] That is, despite the harasser's *intent,* if the conduct has the *effect* of creating a hostile work environment for an employee, that employee's perception is the standard by which the conduct is to be measured. While the harasser may not have meant to cause that effect, the employer may still be liable for his conduct.

Several courts have upheld this standard of proof in sexual harassment cases. In *Bundy v. Jackson*[7] the court focused on the "psychological and emotional" impact that the sexual harassment had on the victim. The court found that the actions did her "serious emotional harm" and "caused her anxiety and debilitation."[8] In *Ferguson v. Dupont*[9] the court concluded that the statements made by the supervisor were "sexist and abusive and were so perceived by the plaintiff."[10] Furthermore in *Ferguson,* the court found that the employer acted on a complaint even though the employer's investigator "felt that such (sexist) conduct was uncharacteristic of the supervisors," the investigator "was willing to assume it had occurred for the purposes of his investigation."[11]

In *Caldwell v. Hodgeman*[12] the court found "judicial vindication" for the EEOC guidelines' view in *Bundy v. Jackson* and welcomed a standard that inquired into the state of mind of the person against whom the sexual conduct is directed. The court wrote:

> Concern with the state of mind of the victim obviates the need to pass judgment upon the seriousness or culpabilities or intentions of the harasser.[13]

Finally, in *Lamb v. Drilco Div.*[14] the court looked to the physical effect that the sexual harassment had on the plaintiff, finding that her job performance deteriorated and she could not eat, sleep or concentrate. Eventually, she began to drink more alcohol than usual.[15]

But court decisions in *Rabidue v. Osceola Refining Co.,*[16] portend a different analysis in the courts of what is unwelcome, at least in hostile work environment cases.

These two courts adopted a different standard for measuring whether the sexual conduct was unwelcome. The appellate court in *Rabidue* described it.

> To accord appropriate protection to both plaintiffs and defendants in a hostile and/or abusive work environment sexual harassment case, the trier of fact, when judging the totality of the circumstances . . . must adopt the perspective of a reasonable person's reaction to a similar environment under essentially like or similar circumstances.[17]

The court continued:

> Thus, in the absence of conduct which would interfere with that hypothetical reasonable individual's work performance and affect seriously the psychological well-being of that reasonable person under like circumstances, a plaintiff may not prevail on . . . charges . . . of a hostile . . . work environment regardless of whether the plaintiff was actually offended by the defendant's conduct.[18]

After a plaintiff proves that such conduct did interfere with her working environment, she must also "demonstrate that she was actually offended by the defendant's conduct and that she suffered some degree of injury as a result of the abusive and hostile environment," the court wrote.[19]

Applying this standard to the facts in *Rabidue,* the appellate court found that the "obscene and vulgar" language of a supervisor "although annoying" was not so "startling as to have affected seriously the psyches of the plaintiff or other female employees."[20] Furthermore, the sexually oriented posters of nude and partially clad women that plaintiff's male co-workers displayed in the workplace

> ". . . had a de minimis effect on the plaintiff's work environment when considered in the context of a society that condones and publicly features and commercially exploits open displays of written and pictorial erotica at the newsstands, on prime-time television, at the cinema and in other public places."[21]

The appellate court in *Rabidue* essentially affirmed the district court's rationale and conclusion that this behavior by a supervisor, who the district court characterized as a "crude and vulgar man"[22] and the posters of nude and partially clad women which the district court noted, the plaintiff saw "during many work days"[23] did not constitute sexual harassment under Title VII.

Judge Keith, who dissented on the three-judge panel in the appellate court, bitterly attacked the decision of the majority. He found that the majority failed to see how the "overall circumstances" of plaintiff's workplace "envinced an anti-female environment."[24] In his review of the court record, Judge Keith found that the one supervisor in question regularly "spewed" anti-female obscenities, including referring to women as "whore," "cunt," "pussy," and "tits."[25] He also noted that the plaintiff had, for seven years, been exposed daily, along with other female workers, to displays in common work areas of nude or partially clad women belonging to male employees. "One poster," he wrote, "which remained on the wall for eight years, showed a prone woman who had a golf ball on her breasts with a man standing over her, a golf club in hand, yelling 'fore.' "[26]

Furthermore, Judge Keith found the female employees were accorded secondary status in the employer's workplace, repeatedly undermined and denied job fringe benefits that were given to men, including free lunches and gasoline, company telephone credit cards and entertainment privileges. Judge Keith concluded that this proved that the employer's supervisors had a "primitive" view of women and an "anti-female animus."[27]

In light of this evidence, Judge Keith adopted a "reasonable woman's" standard in judging the offensiveness of this conduct because, he argued, the "reasonable person's" standard applied by the majority "failed to account for the wide divergence between most women's views of appropriate sexual conduct and those of men."[28] He wrote:

> Unless the outlook of the reasonable woman is adopted, the defendants as well as the courts are permitted to sustain ingrained notions of reasonable behaviors fashioned by the offenders, in this case, men.[29]

But despite the warning in Judge Keith's dissent in *Rabidue* of the danger of applying a "reasonable person's" standard in sexual harassment cases, the majority opinion is a standard by which other courts will measure acts of sexual conduct in the future. The two courts that have already done so, found no violation of Title VII.[30] Others will follow because determining if sexual harassment is "unwelcome" is an essential element in establishing a *prima facie* case and a controversial question of whether an objective or subjective standard is to be applied.

FOOTNOTES

[1] 33 FEP Cases 716, (E.D. Mich. 1982).
[2] *Id.* at 720.
[3] *Id.*
[4] *Id.* at 725.
[5] *Id.*
[6] 29 C.F.R. Section 1604.11(a)(3).
[7] 641 F.2d 934, 24 FEP Cases 1155 (D.C. Cir. 1981).
[8] *Id.* at 1158.
[9] 560 F. Supp 1172, 31 FEP Cases 795 (D. Del. 1983).
[10] *Id.* at 800.
[11] *Id.*
[12] 25 FEP Cases 1647 (D.C. Mass. 1981).
[13] *Id.* at 1649.
[14] 32 FEP Cases 105 (S.D. Tex. 1983).
[15] *Id.* at 106.
[16] 805 F.2d 611, 42 FEP Cases 631 (6th Cir. 1986) *affirming*, 584 F. Supp. 419, 36 FEP Cases 183 (E.D. Mich. 1984).
[17] *Id.* at 638.
[18] *Id.*
[19] *Id.*
[20] *Id.* at 639.
[21] *Id.*
[22] *Id.* at 185.
[23] *Id.*
[24] *Id.* at 640.
[25] *Id.* at 641.
[26] *Id.*
[27] *Id.* at 642.
[28] *Id.* at 642.
[29] *Id.*
[30] See *Highlander v. KFC National Management Co.*, 805 F.2d 644, 42 FEP Cases 654 (6th Cir. 1986) and *Williams-Hill v. Donovan*, 43 FEP Cases 253 (M.D. Fla. 1987).

§2:15. —The Sexual Harassment Was Based On Sex.

This element is derived from the essence of a disparate treatment claim under Title VII that an employee or applicant is intentionally singled out for adverse treatment on the basis of a prohibited criteria.[1]

In a sexual harassment case, a plaintiff must show that but for her sex, she would not have been the object of harassment.[2]

However, there may be a case in which a supervisor makes sexual advances to employees of both sexes or where the conduct complained of is equally offensive to male and female workers.[3]

In such a case, the courts have cautioned that the sexual harassment may not be based on sex because men and women have been treated alike. The appellate court in *Rabidue v. Osceola Refining Co.,*[4] reiterated that warning specifically in a hostile work environment case. To date, in no reported case of sexual harassment, has a court ever denied a sexual harassment cause of action because the facts of the case have shown that both men and women were sexually harassed by the same employee or by different employees but in the same workplace. The *Bundy* court believes that such a situation will never occur. It rejects the argument

> . . . that sexual harassment could not be gender discrimination simply because a woman could also harass a man, or because any homosexual supervisor could harass an employee of the same gender. We noted that in each instance the question is one of but-for causation: would the complaining employee have suffered the harassment had he or she been of a different gender? . . . Only by a *reductio ad absurdum* could we imagine a case of harassment that is not sex discrimination—where a bisexual supervisor harasses men and women alike.[5]

FOOTNOTES

[1] *Henson v. City of Dundee,* 682 F.2d 897, 29 FEP Cases 787, 793 (11th Cir. 1982); *Furnco Construction Corp. v. Waters,* 438 U.S. 567, 577, 98 S. Ct. 2943, 2949, 57 L.Ed. 2d 957, 17 FEP Cases 1062 (1978); *United States v. International Brotherhood of Teamsters,* 431 U.S. 324, 335, n. 15, 97 S. Ct. 1843, 1854 n. 15, 52 L.Ed. 2d 396, 14 FEP Cases 1514 (1977).

[2] *Henson, supra; Bundy v. Jackson,* 641 F. 2d 934 at 942–43, 24FEP Cases 1155 (D.C. Cir. 1981), which cites *Phillips v. Martin Marietta Corp.,* 400 U.S. 542, 91 S. Ct. 496, 27 L.Ed. 2d 613, 3 FEP Cases 40 (1971); *Tomkins v. Public Service Electric and Gas Co.,* 568 F. 2d 1044, 1047 n. 4, 16 FEP Cases 22 (3rd Cir. 1977); Note, "Sexual Harassment and Title VII," U. Mich. L. Rev. 1007, 1019–20 n. 94 (1978), citing *McDonald v. Santa Fe Trail Transportation Co.,* 427 U.S. 273, 282 n. 10, 96 S. Ct. 2574, 2579 n. 10, 49 L.Ed. 2d 493, 12 FEP Cases 1577 (1976).

[3] This possibility is noted in *Henson,* at 793, and in a footnote in *Barnes v. Costle,* 561 F.2d 983, 990 n. 55, 15 FEP Cases 345 (D.C. Cir. 1977).

See also *Bradford v. Sloan,* 8 FEP Cases 634 (N.D. Ala. 1974), where employer did not violate Title VII where manager mistreated white and black employees equally.

[4] 805 F.2d 611, 42 FEP Cases 631, 632 (6th Cir. 1986).

[5] 641 F. 2d 934, 24 FEP Cases 1155, at 1159.

§2:16. ——Effect of Conduct on Terms or Conditions of Employment.

This is a critical element, one which many plaintiff cases have failed to meet because several courts have not found that the sexual harassment complained of was sufficiently connected to the workplace. The language of Title VII specifically refers to discrimination against an individual "with respect to his compensation, terms, conditions or privileges of employment."[1]

In early reported cases of sexual harassment, the courts found no connection between the allegations of sexual harassment and the workplace. In *Corne v. Bausch & Lomb,*[2] the court ruled that "nothing in Title VII prohibits verbal and physical advances where the conduct has "no relationship to the nature of the employment."[3]

Later, the courts rejected that notion and found that the employee's acceptance or refusal of sexual advances was an express or implied condition of receiving a job benefit or avoiding a job detriment.[4] The U. S. Supreme Court in *Meritor Savings Bank v. Vinson*[5] affirmed this determination when it wrote: "Without question, when a supervisor sexually harasses a subordinate because of the subordinate's sex, that supervisor discriminates on the basis of sex."[6]

Thus, proof that the response of a plaintiff in a *quid pro quo* sexual harassment case had an effect on a "term, condition or privilege" of employment is adequate to establish this element of the *prima facie* case. However, in a hostile work environment, the proof is that the sexual harassment *itself* had such an effect.

That is because in a hostile work environment case, proof of a tangible job detriment is not required in order for a "term, condition or privilege" of employment to be affected.[7] Since *Bundy*, other courts have recognized that sexual harassment that creates a hostile work environment does cause "serious emotional harm" and that "conditions of employment" under Title VII do include the "psychological and emotional work environment."[8]

However, the courts have held that a claim of sexual harassment must be "sufficiently severe and persistent to affect seriously the psychological well being of employees."[9] (See previous discussion in this chapter on sexual harassment cases where acts have and have not been sufficiently "severe and persistent.") This determination of "sufficiency" turns on "totality of circumstances."[10]

The court in *Downes v. F.A.A.* also adds that a plaintiff must show that the conduct alleged to have created a hostile work environment has been repeated to the point where it is "routine" or "of a generalized nature" as to "become a condition of anyone's employment."[11] In *Bundy v. Jackson* and *Jordan v. Wilson*[12] the courts characterized this kind of pervasiveness by finding that sexual harassment against women in these two workplaces was "standard operating procedure."

However, it is important to consider a recent ruling in *Rabidue v. Osecola Refining Co.*,[13] where the appellate court sets a "reasonable person's" standard by which the effect of the sexual harassment on a plaintiff's work environment will be judged.[14] That determination may also take into consideration the "personality of the plaintiff and the prevailing work environment," the nature of alleged harassment, background and experience of the plaintiff, and, the court wrote, "the lexicon of obscenity that pervaded the environment of the workplace both before and after the plaintiff's introduction into its environs, coupled with the reasonable expectation of the plaintiff upon voluntarily entering that environment."[15] How this court ruling will influence future cases is not yet known. (See earlier discussion of this case in this chapter.)

Footnotes

[1] 42 U.S.C. Section 2000e–2(a)(1).

[2] 390 F. Supp. 161, 10 FEP Cases 289 (D.C. Ariz. 1975).

[3] *Id.* at 163.

[4] *Williams v. Saxbe,* 413 F. Supp. 654, 12 FEP Cases 1093 (D.D.C. 1976).

[5] —U.S.—, 106 S. Ct. 2399, 2404, 40 FEP Cases 1822 (1986).

[6] *Id.* at 2404.

[7] *Bundy v. Jackson,* 641 F.2d 934, 24 FEP Cases 1155 (D.C. Cir. 1981).

[8] *Meritor Savings Bank,* 106 S.Ct. at 2405; *Henson v. City of Dundee,* 682 F.2d 897, 29 FEP Cases 787 (11th Cir. 1982); *Coley v. Consolidated Rail Corp.,* 561 F. Supp. 645, 34 FEP Cases 129, (E. D. Mich. 1982). See also *Rogers v. EEOC,* 454 F.2d 234. 4 FEP Cases 92 (5th Cir. 1971), *cert. denied,* 406 U. S. 957, 4 FEP Cases 471 (1972).

[9] *Henson,* 29 FEP Cases at 793–94.

[10] *Downes v. F.A.A.,* 39 FEP Cases 70, 775 F. 2d 288 (Fed. Cir. 1985) (1985). See also EEOC guidelines on sexual harassment, 29 C.F.R. Section 1604.11(b).

[11] *Downes,* 39 FEP Cases at 75.

[12] 649 F. Supp. 1038, 42 FEP Cases 950, 965 (D. C. Ala. 1986).

[13] 805 F.2d 611, 42 FEP Cases 631 (6th Cir. 1986), *affirming,* 584 F.Supp 419, 36 FEP Cases 183 (E. D. Mich 1984).

[14] *Id.* at 638.

[15] *Id.*

§2:17. —Respondeat Superior.

A final element of a *prima facie* case of sexual harassment is a determination of the employer's responsibility for the actions of its employees that may constitute sexual harassment. Respondeat superior is a legal theory that makes an employer (company) responsible for the actions of its employees (supervisors). It is not the individual supervisor, but the employer who is sued.

Several courts have labeled this the most critical element of the *prima facie* case because the order of proof for disparate treatment cases has been modified in sexual harassment cases to eliminate proof of intent to discriminate. In *Katz v. Dole,*[1] the court noted that, since any act of sexual harassment was "an intentional assault on an individual's innermost privacy," once the plaintiff proves that the harassment took place, "the most difficult legal question typically will concern the responsibility of the employer for that harassment." The plaintiff will have to demonstrate that the employer is liable under some theory of *respondeat superior.*[2]

FOOTNOTES

[1] 709 F. 2d 251, 31 FEP Cases 1521, 1524 (4th Cir. 1983).

[2] *Id.* at 1523–1524.

§2:18. Other Causes of Action.

One court has recognized a cause of action for non-sexual physical assault even though the EEOC guidelines on sexual harassment define sexual harassment as ". . . physical conduct of a sexual nature."[1] In *McKinney v. Dole*[2] the appellate court ruled that "a physically aggressive but not explicitly sexual act" by her male supervisor against a female employee did violate Title VII. This act involved a male supervisor grabbing the plaintiff's arm and twisting it. The assault exacerbated an earlier, unrelated injury.

The defendant employer argued in the district court that since there was no sexual connotations to this incident nor was it "any attempt to obtain or to coerce the plaintiff to engage in any form of sexual act," it was not illegal sexual harassment.[3] The district court agreed and ruled that the plaintiff had no cause of action for sexual harassment under Title VII "because she failed to allege facts . . . which would create a genuine issue of discrimination based on sex."[4]

On appeal, the Circuit Court of Appeals for the District of Columbia rejected the defendant's argument that the alleged assault "was simply violent and did not include overt sexual advances or suggestions"[5] and criticized "as legally flawed" the district court's assumption that

> an incident of physical force toward an employee by a supervisor cannot constitute sexual discrimination or harassment unless it is for the purpose of obtaining sexual favors or is otherwise blatantly sexually oriented.[6]

The appellate court reversed the district court and ruled:

> We have never held that sexual harassment or other unequal treatment of an employee or group of employees that occurs because of the sex of the employee must, to be illegal under Title VII, take the form of sexual advances or of other incidents with clearly sexual overtones. And we decline to do so now. Rather, we hold that any harassment or other unequal treatment of an employee or group of employees that would not occur but for the sex of the employee or employees may, if sufficiently patterned or pervasive comprise an illegal condition of employment under Title VII.

FOOTNOTES

[1] 29 C.F.R. 1604.11 (a).

[2] 765 F.2d 1129, 38 FEP Cases 364, 365 (D.C. Cir. 1985).

[3] *Id.* at 369.

[4] *Id.* at 370.

[5] *Id.* at 370.

[6] *Id.* at 370.

§2:19. Summary.

A plaintiff must establish a *prima facie* case of sexual harassment by alleging and proving certain essential elements, which taken together, constitute sexual harassment. Similar proof required in both a *quid pro quo* and a hostile work environment cases of sexual harassment. Each case requires proof of a critical element—finding the employer responsible for the sexual harassment under *respondeat superior.* Because this is an important element, it will be explored in more detail in the next chapter.

CHAPTER THREE

Employer Liability for Sexual Harassment

§3:01. Overview.

One of the most hotly contested legal questions in sexual harassment litigation today is "When is an employer liable for illegal sexual conduct in the workplace?"

Not surprisingly, this is "the most difficult legal question" in a sexual harassment case.[1] It is also an important element of the *prima facie* case which a plaintiff must establish.[2] That element of proof requires finding the employer responsible for the sexual harassment under *respondeat superior.*

Respondeat superior is a legal theory based on common-law agency principles that an employer (the company) is liable for the actions of its employees (e.g. supervisors or agents). Under Title VII, "employers" are prohibited from discriminating against any individual "with respect to his compensation, terms, conditions or privileges of employment . . . because of . . . sex."[3] The statutory definition of "employer" includes "any agent of such person."[4] Under Title VII, it is the employer, not the individual supervisor, who is sued for employment discrimination. (But see discussion of liability of individual supervisors later in this chapter.) Several courts have ruled that an employer is responsible for the discriminatory acts of its agents under Title VII.[5]

In sexual harassment cases, the courts have grappled with how an employer is liable for the sexual conduct of its employees. In the first reported federal sexual harassment decision, *Corne v. Bausch & Lomb*,[6] the court held that the employer was not liable when it had no company policy *condoning* sexual harassment. The court cited cases in which employer rules were found to be discriminatory, e.g. an employer's rule that denies employment to married women and which is not applicable to married men, *Sprogis v. United Airlines, Inc.*,[7] but distinguished those cases when it wrote:

> the discriminatory conduct complained of, arose out of company policies. There was apparently some advantage to, or gain by, the employer from such discriminatory practices. Always such discriminatory practices were employer designed and oriented. In the present case, . . . no employer policy is . . . involved; rather than the company being benefited, in any way by the conduct of (the supervisor), it is obvious it can only be damaged by the very nature of the acts complained of.[8]

The lower court decision in *Corne* was vacated and remanded on appeal,[9] but one court adopted its reasoning. In *Ludington v. Sambo's Restaurants, Inc.*[10] the court ruled that acts alleged, "obscene and vulgar suggestions" and "physical contact" by a manager,[11] were not sexual harassment because the employer "did not sanction" such conduct.[12] The court decision does not eludicate in what way an employer could do so.

Other court decisions after *Corne* noted the absurdity of that case's reasoning and conclusion. In *Heelan v. Johns-Manville Corp.*,[13] the court wrote:

> It is not necessary for a plaintiff to prove a policy or practice of the employer endorsing sexual harassment . . . To demand that a plaintiff prove a company-directed policy of sexual discrimination is merely to extend a claim for relief with one hand and take it away with the other. In no other area of employment discrimination do the courts require such proof. See e.g. *Ostapowicz v. Johnson Bronze Co.*, 369 F. Supp. 522 (W. D. Pa. 1973).[14]

On the other hand, in *Miller v. Bank of America,*[15] the lower court ruled that the employer was not liable when it had a policy *against* sexual harassment and the plaintiff did not use that policy to complain within the company before filing a federal lawsuit. On appeal, the Ninth Circuit Court of Appeals reversed that finding and held that

> . . . *respondeat superior* does apply here, where the action complained of was that of a supervisor, authorized to hire, fire, discipline or promote, or at least to participate in or recommend such actions, even though what the supervisor is said to have done violates company policy.[16]

The 1980 guidelines on sexual harassment of the federal Equal Employment Opportunity Commission (EEOC) affirm this view of liability in a sexual harassment case. The guidelines read in part, "an employer . . . is responsible for its acts and those of its agents and supervisory employees with respect to sexual harassment regardless of whether the specific acts complained of were authorized or even forbidden by the employer. . . ."[17]

The appellate court in *Miller* also disagreed with the lower court's finding that an employee alleging sexual harassment must first use a company's internal grievance procedure. The court said, "We decline to read an exhaustion of company remedies requirement into Title VII."[18] In so concluding, the appellate court in *Miller* relied on the U.S. Supreme Court decision in *McDonnell Douglas Corp. v. Green,*[19] where it found that Title VII does not "restrict a complainant's right to sue."[20] It relied, too, on established Title VII case law that an employee need not exhaust union remedies as a prerequisite to a Title VII suit. The U.S. Supreme Court wrote in *Alexander v. Gardner-Denver Co.,*[21] "[a]n employee's Title VII rights are independent of contractual rights."

Thus, while initially the courts did not find an employer liable under *respondeat superior* in sexual harassment cases, these decisions were reversed on appeal or criticized by courts in subsequent decisions where such liability was found. Gradually, the courts began to look at the issue of employer liability under *respondeat superior* in light of the answers to three specific questions. Did the employer know about the sexual harassment? Was the harasser a supervisor or co-worker? Do the plaintiff's allegations involve *quid pro quo* or hostile work environment sexual harassment?

This chapter will explore how the courts have formulated rules of liability in sexual harassment cases based on the answers to these questions. These rules govern what a plaintiff must prove in order to establish the fifth element of her *prima facie* case: The employer was liable for the sexual harassment under *respondeat superior.*

FOOTNOTES

[1] *Katz v. Dole,* 709 F.2d 251, 31 FEP Cases 1521, 1524 (4th Cir. 1983).

[2] *Heelan v. Johns-Manville Corp.,* 451 F. Supp. 1382, 20 FEP Cases 251 (D. Col. 1978); *Henson v. City of Dundee,* 682 F. 2d 897, 29 FEP Cases 787 (11th Cir. 1982).

[3] 42 U.S.C. Section 2000e-2(a)(1).

[4] 42 U.S.C. Section 2000e(b).

[5] *Young v. Southwestern Sav. & Loan Ass'n,* 509 F.2d 140, 144 n. 7 (5th Cir. 1975); *Tidwell v. American Oil Co.,* 332 F. Supp. 424 (D. Utah 1971); *Anderson v. Methodist Evangelical Hospital, Inc.,* 464 F.2d 723, 725, 4 FEP Cases 987, 988 (6th Cir. 1972); *Calcote v. Texas Educational Foundation,* 578 F.2d 95, 98, 20 FEP Cases 1685 (5th Cir. 1978); *Friend v. Leidinger,* 88 F.2d 61, 69, 18 FEP Cases 1052 (4th Cir. 1978).

[6] 390 F. Supp. 161, 10 FEP Cases 289 (D.C. Ariz. 1975).

[7] 444 F.2d 1194, 3 FEP Cases 621 (7th Cir. 1971).

[8] 390 F. Supp. 161, 10 FEP Cases 289, at 290–291.

[9] 562 F 2d. 55, 15 FEP Cases 1370 (4th Cir., 1977).

[10] 474 F. Supp. 480, 20 FEP Cases 1000 (E. D. Wisc. 1979).

[11] *Id.* at 1002.

[12] *Id.* at 1003.

[13] 451 F. Supp. 1382, 20 FEP Cases 251 (D. Colorado, 1978).

[14] *Id.* at 1389.

[15] 418 F. Supp 233, 13 FEP Cases 439 (N. D. Calif. 1976).

[16] 600 F.2d 211, 20 FEP Cases 462, 464 (9th Cir. 1979).

[17] 29 C.F. R. Section 1604.11(c).

[18] 600 F. 2d 211, 20 FEP Cases 462, at 464.

[19] 411 U. S. 792, 93 S. Ct. 1817, 36 L. Ed. 2d 668, 5 FEP Cases 965 (1981).

[20] *Id.* at 798.

[21] 415 U. S. 36, 49–50, 94 S. Ct. 1011, 39 L. Ed. 2d 147, 7 FEP Cases 81, 87 (1974).

§3:02. The Employer's Knowledge of Sexual Harassment.

The first question—Did the employer know about the sexual harassment?—is concerned with how an employer learns about sexual harassment in its workplace. The courts have indicated two ways in which an employer can gain such knowledge. First, there may be "actual knowledge," that is an employee complains directly to a supervisor, manager or some employee who is charged with insuring that there is equal employment opportunity in the workplace (e.g. an affirmative action officer or member of the personnel staff). In *Bundy v. Jackson,*[1] the plaintiff complained to the superior of the two supervisors who were sexually harassing her, then to other individuals including the EEOC officer and finally, the director of the agency.[2] The court found that the employer had "full knowledge of the alleged offense."[3]

An employer can also have "constructive knowledge" of the sexual harassment. This occurs when an employer "should" have known of the occurrence of the acts in the circumstances of the case. In *Henson v. City of Dundee,*[4] the court recognized that this notice may be given "by showing the pervasiveness of the harassment, . . . which gives rise to the inference of knowledge or constructive knowledge."[5] In *Taylor,* the plaintiff alleged that she had been subjected to racial epithets and slurs and that she resigned from her job because of the "noxious" racial atmosphere in the workplace.[6] The appellate court found "ample evidence" in the lower court record that the racial atmosphere was "dismal" and that "the atmosphere of racial discrimination and of prejudice was so pervasive and so long continuing . . . that the employer must have been conscious of it."[7]

But how an employer gains knowledge in a sexual harassment case is only important if the knowledge is required in order for the employer to be held responsible for sexual harassment. In some sexual harassment cases, the employer has been held to a standard of "strict liability." In such a case, it is not a defense that the employer had no knowledge. On the other hand, if knowledge is required, a plaintiff must allege and prove that the employer had either actual or constructive knowledge of the sexual harassment, and took no corrective action.

Footnotes

[1] 641 F 2d. 934, 24 FEP Cases 1155 (D. C. Cir. 1981).

[2] *Id.* at 1157–1158.

[3] *Id.* at 1159, n. 8.

[4] 682 F. 2d 897, 29 FEP Cases 787 (11th Cir. 1982).

[5] *Id.* at 794, citing *Taylor v. Jones,* 653 F. 2d 1193, 1199, 28 FEP Cases 1024 (8th Cir. 1981).

[6] *Id.* at 1025.

[7] *Id.* at 1027.

See also *Katz v. Dole;* 1709 F.2d 251, 31 FEP Cases 1521, 1524 (4th Cir. 1983) where the court held that the sexual harassment was "so pervasive that employer awareness may be inferred."

§3:03. The Position of the Harasser.

The second question—Was the harasser a supervisor or co-worker?—considers the position of the alleged harasser in relation to the plaintiff in the workplace. The courts have generally found that in order to be an "employer" for the purpose of Title VII, an individual must be an officer, director or supervisor of a Title VII employer, or otherwise involved in managerial decisions.[1]

Supervisors are those individuals who have the power to hire, fire, discipline or promote subordinates.[2] Co-workers, on the other hand, do not exercise such powers over other co-workers, although some may also have supervisory functions. When that occurs, the courts have held co-workers to the standard of liability for a supervisor.[3]

The EEOC guidelines on sexual harassment indicate that the "Commission will examine the circumstances of the particular employment relationship and the job functions performed by the individual acts in either a supervisory or agency capacity."[4]

Footnotes

[1] *Hendrix v. Fleming Cos.*, 650 F. Supp. 301, 42 FEP Cases 461 (W. D. Oklahoma 1986); *Jeter v. Boswell,* 554 F. Supp. 946, 33 FEP Cases 1410 (N. D. W. Va. 1983); *Guyette v. Stauffer Chemical Co.*, 518 F. Supp. 521, 26 FEP Cases 634 (D. N.J. 1981); *EEOC v. Charleston Elec. Joint Apprenticeship,* 587 F. Supp. 528, 35 FEP Cases 473 (S.D. W. Va. 1984); *Tafoya v. Adams,* 612 F. Supp. 1097, 38 FEP Cases 630 (D. Colo. 1985); *Weaver v. Gross,* 605 F. Supp. 210, 37 FEP Cases 1602 (D. D. C. 1985).

[2] *Miller v. Bank of America,* 600 F.2d 211, 20 FEP Cases 462 (9th Cir. 1979).

[3] See *Robson v. Evds Supermarket,* 538 F. Supp. 857, 30 FEP Cases 1213, 1217 (N. D. Ohio, 1982).

[4] 29 C.F.R. 1604.11 (c).

§3:04. The Form of Sexual Harassment.

The final question is what form of sexual harassment has been alleged by the plaintiff. One form is *quid pro quo* in which a plaintiff claims that sexual advances have been made and rejected and she has suffered some employment consequence (e.g. she has been fired, not promoted, demoted or lost her job).[1] The other form is hostile work environment, where the sexual conduct falls short of causing the plaintiff a tangible job detriment, but she has been subjected to sexual harassment that creates "a hostile, intimidating or offensive work environment."[2]

The EEOC guidelines on sexual harassment recognize both forms of sexual harassment.[3] But when the guidelines set forth employer liability, the deciding factor is not what form of sexual harassment has occurred, but whether the harasser is a supervisor or co-worker. The guidelines set forth the following rules:

1. An employer is responsible for the acts of its *supervisory employees,* regardless of whether the employer knew or should have known of their occurrence. (i.e. strict liability)
2. An employer is responsible for the acts of *fellow employees* where the employer (or its agents or supervisory employees) knows or should have known of the conduct, unless it can show that it took immediate corrective action.[4]

While EEOC guidelines do not have the force of law, the courts have deferred to them in resolving many issues in sexual harassment cases.[5]

However, the EEOC guidelines' view of employer liability in sexual harassment cases involving supervisors has been most controversial. Court rulings in *quid pro quo* sexual harassment cases prior to the issuance of the EEOC guidelines in 1980 did not apply a strict liability standard for acts of a supervisor and focused on how an employer can be relieved of responsibility with notice and corrective action. In later cases, the courts have split about whether to adopt the strict liability rule in both *quid pro quo* and hostile work environment cases involving supervisors. This development of caselaw will be explored below by discussing an employer's liability for the acts of supervisors under each form of sexual harassment.

FOOTNOTES

[1] See *William v. Saxbe,* 413 F. Supp. 654, 12 FEP Cases 1093 (D.C.C. 1976).

[2] See *Bundy v. Jackson,* 641 F.2d 934, 24 FEP Cases 1155 (D.C. Cir. 1981).

[3] 29 C.F. R. Section 1604.11(a).

[4] Derived from 29 C.F.R. Section 1604.11(c) and (d).

[5] *Meritor Savings Bank v. Vinson,* —U. S.—, 106 S. Ct. 2399, 2405, 40 FEP Cases 1822 (1986); *Downes v. F.A.A.,* 775 F.2d 288, 291, 39 FEP Cases 70 (Fed. Cir. 1985); *Henson v. City of Dundee,* 682 F.2d 897, 29 FEP Cases 787 (11th Cir. 1982); *Bundy v. Jackson,* 641 F.2d 934, 947, 24 FEP Cases 1155 (D. C. Cir. 1981); *Walter v. KFGO Radio,* 518 F. Supp. 1309, 1315, 26 FEP Cases 982 (D. N.D. 1981).

See generally *General Electric Co. v. Gilbert,* 429 U. S. 125, 140–45, 97 S. Ct. 401, 410–12, 50 L. Ed. 2d 343, 13 FEP Cases 1657 (1976).

§3:05. Employer Liability for Supervisor Acts in Quid Pro Quo Cases.

Several court decisions, all prior to the issuance of the EEOC guidelines, hold the employer to a standard of liability for the supervisor's acts but recognize that the employer can be relieved of responsibility, if, when notified, the situation is remedied. In

Tomkins v. Public Service Electric & Gas,[1] the court concluded that Title VII is violated

> when a supervisor, with the actual or constructive knowledge of the employer, makes sexual advances or demands toward a subordinate employee and conditions that employee's job status . . . on a favorable response . . . and the employer does not take prompt and appropriate remedial action.

In *Barnes v. Costle,*[2] the court wrote, "We realize that should a supervisor contravene employer policy without the employer's knowledge, and the consequences are rectified when discovered, the employer may be relieved from responsibility under Title VII."[3]

In *Miller v. Bank of America,*[4] the district court found the employer was not liable for the sexual harassment because the plaintiff did not complain under the company's existing internal grievance procedure and the company had a policy expressly condemning sexual harassment.

Several subsequent court decisions cite *Tomkins, Barnes* and *Miller* for the proposition that that liability is *negated* if the employer has knowledge of sexual harassment and does not act to correct it. In *Heelan v. Johns-Manville Corp.,*[5] the court ruled that "if an employer is aware of the situation and rectifies it, the employer may not be held liable for the acts of its agent."[6] In *Meyers v. I.T.T. Diversified Credit Corp.,*[7] the court held the employer liable because it had actual knowledge of the supervisor's actions and failed to rectify the situation, citing *Heelan, Tomkins* and *Miller.*[8]

These courts have also taken the rulings in *Tomkins, Barnes* and *Miller* to require that notice must be given *before* an employer is liable for the sexual harassment. In *Heelan* and *Lamb,* the courts do not necessarily suggest that such notice is necessary, but in *Meyers,* the court is more explicit:

> The last element of the *prima facie* case that plaintiff had to establish in order to impose liability on the defendant . . . is that the defendant had

> knowledge or constructive knowledge of the discriminatory acts of its officer manager.[9]

But a reading of the subsequent court analysis of the decisions in *Tomkins, Barnes* and *Miller* indicates that these cases did not intend to extend the liability rule in that way. The *Miller* decision was squarely reversed on appeal on the issue of whether an employee was required to file a complaint.[10] The appellate court wrote, "we decline to read an exhaustion of company remedies requirement into Title VII."[11] Therefore, on appeal, the *Miller* court decision endorsed the strict liability rule.

The *Tomkins* ruling by the Third Circuit Court of Appeals was later clarified by that same court in *Craig v. Y & Y Snacks.*[12] There the court found that the employee had notified the employer after she suspected she had been fired for spurning the sexual advances of her supervisor and that notice squared with *Tomkins.*

> . . . (the employer) had actual notice of the harassment immediately after the discharge and failed to take adequate remedial steps. Actual knowledge at the time of the employment decision at issue satisfies the *Tomkins* ruling.[13]

But then the appellate court went on in *Craig* to note that "when a supervisor who has plenary authority over hiring, discipline and dismissal makes an employment decision, that decision may be imputed to the employer,"[14] citing several racial discrimination cases. Then it concluded:

> the imputation of knowledge to an employer in situations such as this one, in which an offending supervisor has unbridled authority to retaliate against an employee is in accord with *Tomkins.*[15]

This discussion in *Craig* of the court's earlier ruling was seen as a "redefinition" of the *Tomkins* decision in *Horn v. Duke Homes.*[16] The *Horn* court found that in *Craig,* the Third Circuit Court "redefined the 'constructive' knowledge component in a way that allowed the court to shift from a fault-based liability to one of strict liability." The appellate court in *Craig* also cited with approval, as the *Horn* court noted, the strict liability rules of the other circuits, including *Henson* for the Eleventh Circuit and *Miller* for the Ninth Circuit.[17]

Finally, the decision of the Circuit Court of Appeals for the District of Columbia in *Barnes v. Costle* was further explained by that same court in *Vinson v. Taylor.*[18] The appellate court was concerned that the *Vinson* district court relied on a statement made in *Barnes v. Costle* that "should a supervisor contravene employer policy without the employer's knowledge and the consequences are rectified when discovered, the employer may be relieved from responsibility under Title VII."[19] The appellate court in *Vinson* warned:

> That statement should not be laden with a significance beyond its function merely as an acknowledgement of holdings in the two cases we there cited. One of those cases, *Miller v. Bank of America,* 418 F. Supp. 233, 13 FEP Cases 439 (N. D. Cal. 1976), was subsequently reversed on appeal. . . . the other . . . concerned racial slurs, not by supervisory personnel but co-workers, who differ radically from supervisors in the scheme of vicarious liability (*Id.*) citing EEOC guidelines, 29 C. F. R. Section 1604.11(c).[20]

In addition, the *Tomkins* and *Barnes* decisions are squarely disputed by the court in *Henson v. City of Dundee.*[21] The court wrote:

> We reject the argument in *Tomkins* that an employer may escape "responsibility" for sexual harassment of this type merely by taking subsequent remedial action. Such action by the employer may, of course, mitigate damages, but it in no way affects an employer's liability.[22]

Likewise, in *Horn v. Duke Homes,*[23] the court found "no support in either precedent or policy" for the employer's contention where actual or constructive knowledge of a supervisor's conduct is required "before holding an employer liable for sexual harassment involving a tangible job detriment."[24]

Thus, the analysis in cases subsequent to *Barnes v. Costle, Tomkins* and *Miller* clarify that an employer is strictly liable in *quid pro quo* sexual harassment cases. The court in *Horn* found ample support in public policy for this rule.

> . . . [S]ex discrimination can best be eradicated by enforcing a strict liability rule that ensures compensation for victims and creates an incentive for the employer to take the strongest possible affirmative measure to prevent the hiring and retention of sexist supervisors.[25]

The court in *Henson v. City of Dundee,*[26] also set forth a reason for the strict liability rule in a *quid pro quo* case.

> In such a case, the supervisor relies upon his apparent or actual authority to extort sexual consideration from an employee. . . . In that case the supervisor uses the means furnished to him by the employer to accomplish the prohibited purpose.

Thus, as to *quid pro quo* sexual harassment cases, the federal courts are now in accord with the EEOC guidelines on sexual harassment,[27] that when supervisors sexually harass a subordinates, liability of the employer is strict liability—whether or not the employer had knowledge. It is still unclear in *quid pro quo* sexual harassment cases after *Henson* if immediate corrective actions by an employer negates liability or merely mitigates damages.

FOOTNOTES

[1] 568 F. Supp. 1044, 1048, 16 FEP Cases 22 (3rd. Cir. 1977).

[2] 561 F.2d. 983, 993, 15 FEP Cases 345, 353 (D.C. Cir. 1977).

[3] See also *Munford v. James T. Barnes & Co.,* 441 F. Supp. 459, 17 FEP Cases 107 (E. D. Mich. 1977).

[4] 418 F. Supp 233, 13 FEP Cases 439 (N.D. Calif. 1976).

[5] 451 F. Supp. 1382, 20 FEP Cases 251 (D. Colo. 1978).

[6] Id. at 255, citing *Barnes v. Costle*, 561 F. 2d 983, 15 FEP Cases 345, 353 (D.C. Cir. 1977).

[7] 542 F. Supp. 123, 27 FEP Cases 995 (E. D. Mo. 1981).

[8] See also *Lamb v. Drilco Div.,* 32 FEP Cases 105, 107 (S. D. Texas, 1983). (Both *Lamb* and *Meyers* were decided after the EEOC guidelines were issued.)

[9] Myers v. ITT Diversified Credit Corp., 542 F. Supp. 123, 27 FED Cases 995, 999 (E.D. Mo. 1981), citing *Tomkins* and *Barnes v. Costle.*

[10] *Miller v. Bank of America,* 600 F.2d 211, 20 FEP Cases 462, 464 (9th Cir. 1979).

[11] *Id.* at 464.

[12] 721 F. 2d 77, 80, 33 FEP Cases 187 (3rd Cir. 1983).

[13] *Id.* at 189.
[14] *Id.* at 189.
[15] *Id.* at 190.
[16] 755 F. 2d 599, 37 FEP Cases 228, 232 n. 7 (7th Cir. 1985).
[17] *Id.*
[18] 753 F.2d 141, 36 FEP Cases 1423, 1428, n. 45 (D.C. Cir. 1985).
[19] 561 F.2d 983 at 993, 15 FEP Cases 345.
[20] *Vinson v. Taylor*, 753 F.2d 141, 36 FEP Cases 1423 (D.C. Cir. 1985).
[21] 682 F.2d 897, 29 FEP Cases 787 (11th Cir. 1982).
[22] *Id.* at 798 n. 19.
[23] 755 F.2d 599, 37 FEP Cases 228 (7th Cir. 1985).
[24] *Id.* at 231.
[25] *Id.* at 232.
[26] 682 F.2d 897, 29 FEP Cases 787 (11th Cir. 1982).
[27] 29 C. F. R. Section 1604.11(c).

§3:06. Hostile Work Environment—Cases Involving Supervisors.

While the EEOC guidelines state that supervisor's actions are always subject to strict liability, some courts have distinguished hostile work environment cases involving supervisors from *quid pro quo* cases. These courts have ruled that an employer is *only* liable for the hostile work environment sexual harassment by supervisors if it knew of the sexual harassment and failed to take immediate corrective action.[1]

The *Henson* court explains its rationale for finding a different standard of liability for hostile environment cases. While it agrees that a supervisor or co-worker can equally create an offensive work environment, the court found that the ability of a worker to create such an environment

> . . . is not necessarily enhanced or diminished by any degree of authority which the employer confers upon that individual. When a supervisor gratuitously insults an employee, he generally does so for his reasons and by his own means. He thus acts outside the actual or apparent scope of the authority he possesses as a supervisor. His conduct cannot be automatically imputed to the employer any more so than can the conduct of an ordinary employee.[2]

The court in *Ferguson* reiterated the *Henson* court's argument that "when supervisory personnel engage in such activity, they act outside the scope of their authority and agency principles therefore do not apply."[3] For that reason, the *Ferguson* court found the strict liability rule of the EEOC guidelines "too onerous a burden" for an employer in a hostile work environment case and followed the rulings of the court in *Henson.*[4]

In addition, in *Ferguson,* the court ruled that the employer was not liable because it took, upon actual knowledge of the sexual harassment (plaintiff complained in writing to the director of her department), "prompt remedial measures and the incidents indisputably stopped."[5] However, it is not clear that the appellate court (11th Circuit) in *Henson* would agree with the 1983 holding of the *Ferguson* district court, that notice and corrective action by the employer *negates* liability. The *Henson* court as noted above, indicated in its 1982 decision that "such action by the employer may, of course, mitigate damages but it in no way affects an employer's liability."[6]

On the other hand, several courts have adopted the strict liability standard of the EEOC guidelines even in hostile work environment cases involving supervisors.[7]

In *Bundy,* the appellate court strongly endorsed the strict liability rule in the EEOC guidelines on sexual harassment,[8] even though in *Bundy,* the employer had actual knowledge of the sexual harassment and took no immediate corrective action.

In *Vinson,* the appellate court reversed the lower court's decision that the employer was not liable because it had no notice of the actions of its supervisor. The court wrote, "We cannot accept this conclusion or its rationale."[9] The appellate court's analysis was that Title VII actually sets "a higher level of imputed responsibility to the employer than *respondeat superior.*"[10]

The court wrote:

> Traditional principles of *respondeat superior,* as they obtain in the field of torts, are not altogether suitable for resolution of questions of Title VII law. The explanation is manifest: Title VII is a mandate from Congress to cure a perceived evil—certain types of discrimination in

employment—in a prescribed fashion. Rules of tort law on the other hand, have evolved over centuries to meet diverse societal demands by allocating risks of harm and duties of care. Without clear congressional instruction, we think it unsafe to rely uncritically on dogma thus begotten.[11]

The court noted that the limitations imposed by the doctrine of *respondeat superior* "have no place in enforcement of congressional will underlying Title VII."[12] The *Vinson* court answered the argument of courts in *Henson* and *Ferguson,* by recognizing that, under the general rules of agency, a master (here, an employer) is not subject to liability for the torts of his servants (supervisors) actions outside the scope of their employment.[13]

But the *Vinson* court emphasized that confining liability in sexual harassment Title VII cases only to situations in which a supervisor had acted within the scope of his authority "conceivably could lead to the ludicrous result that employers would become accountable only if they explicity require or consciously allow their supervisors to molest women employees."[14] The court concluded that "there was no need to so confine either the analysis or the solution where Title VII applies"[15] to common law agency law underlying *respondeat superior.*

To require notice to the employer in a hostile work environment case involving a supervisor, the *Vinson* court said, "is to open the door to circumvention of Title VII by the simple expedient of looking the other way, even as signs of discriminatory practice begin to gather on the horizon," and "create an enormous loophole, one we think that courts should strive to seal."[16] The court added:

Instead of providing a reason for employers to remain oblivious to conditions in the workplace, we think the enlightened purpose of Title VII calls for an interpretation cultivating an incentive for employers to take a more active role in warranting to each employee that he or she will enjoy a working environment free from illegal sex discrimination.[17]

The court explained:

> A requirement of knowledge by the employer of Title VII transgressions by supervisory personnel would effectively eliminate vicarious liability altogether. It would reserve Title VII liability for those employers who fail to redress known violations . . . This would be a retreat from the level of protection Title VII has consistently and designedly afforded and take a backward step we refuse to endorse.[18]

The court concluded:

> A higher level of imputed responsibility than *respondeat superior* imposes is one way to guard against the danger that disobedience of Title VII will escape scrutiny and go unremedied.[19]

The district court in *Jeppsen v. Wunnicke,*[20] endorsed the *Vinson* court's reasoning and conclusion and made two additional points.

First, the *Jeppsen* court acknowledged that requiring knowledge on the part of the employer in a hostile work environment case might very well provide the court "with an easy tool to use in deciding many cases, but this court fears that such a requirement holds the potential for grave injustice as well as subversion of the purpose of Title VII."[21]

The court was concerned with an employee who is "most dependent upon retaining" her job who will not quit because of the sexual harassment or

> Worse yet, this same employee is likely to be the one most reticent to complain, and thereby pass knowledge to a higher supervisor, lest he or she be confronted by the same kind of response that Bundy (in *Bundy v. Jackson*) received when she thought to complain—that is her complaint was not taken seriously, poor performance ratings started appearing, and ultimately a promotion was denied.[2]

Secondly, the *Jeppsen* court pointed out distinction between the two forms of sexual harassment is an "extremely slippery concept."[23] It explained:

> The situations which are dealt with in sex discrimination cases . . . present a factual and legal continuum. There is no neat square peg that fits into a square hole. . . . Rather, there is a seemingly endless variety of sex discrimination cases with one situation blending into another when comparisons are made.[24]

The court concluded:

> This court rejects the notion that a knowledge requirement exists in one situation but not in the other. Preventing sex discrimination in employment is too important a goal to turn upon the vagaries of what does and what does not constitute a *tangible* job benefit as distinguished from what is evidently considered to be an *intangible* benefit such as psychological well-being at the workplace.[25]

The question of employer liability in hostile work environment cases involving supervisors was squarely addressed by the U.S. Supreme Court in the appeal of the *Vinson v. Taylor* case.[26]

To summarize the history of this case, the lower court, ruled[27] prior to *Bundy,* that plaintiff had not proven her *quid pro quo* case because she suffered no tangible job detriment and the employer had no notice of the supervisor's acts. On appeal[28] the court reversed in light of its decision in *Bundy,* holding that the supervisor had created a hostile work environment and the employer was strictly liable for those acts.

In the majority opinion written by Justice Rehnquist, the Court answered the question of whether an employer is strictly liable for an offensive work environment created by a supervisor's actions. "We decline the parties' invitation to issue a definitive rule on employer liability."[29]

The Court's reason for this lack of response was to explain that the "debate over the appropriate standard for employer liability has a rather abstract quality about it given the state of the record of this case."[30] The Court had earlier in its ruling remanded the case to the district court for further findings on whether the sexual harassment was unwelcomed and whether it constituted a "condition of employment" for the plaintiff. Without those findings, the Court found a definitive ruling on employer liability premature.

In *dicta,* however, the decision for the majority of the Court did hint at its position.

First, the Court stated

> "We agree that Congress wanted courts to look to agency principles for guidance in this area. While such common-law principles may not be

> transferable in all their particulars to Title VII, Congress' decision to define "employer" to include any "agent" of an employer, 42 U. S. C. Section 2000e(b), surely envinces an intent to place some limits on the acts of employees for which supervisors under Title VII are to be held responsible.[31]

This statement is a reference back to the appellate court's conclusion in *Vinson v. Taylor,* discussed earlier here, that employer liability under Title VII supersedes common law agency principles. The *Vinson* appellate court found a "higher level of imputed responsibility than respondeat superior" under Title VII.[32] It also refers to the position argued by the Equal Employment Opportunity Commission in its brief to the Supreme Court in *Meritor Savings Bank,* "that the usual basis for finding of agency will often disappear" in a hostile work environment case.[33] The EEOC believed that application of agency principles require the victim of sexual harassment to take advantage of "an avenue of complaint regarding such harassment."[34] If the employee does not do so, "the employer should be shielded from liability, absent actual knowledge."[35]

The Supreme Court, recognizing this EEOC position was in "some tension"[36] with the strict liability rule in its own guidelines,[37] pointed to another part of that section of the guidelines which allow the EEOC to "examine the circumstances of the particular employment relationship and the job [f]unctions performed by the individual in determining whether an individual acts in either a supervisory or agency capacity."[38]

Besides this *dicta,* the Supreme Court did hold in *Meritor Savings Bank* that the Court of Appeals erred in concluding "that employers are always automatically liable for sexual harassment by their supervisors," yet "absence of notice to an employer does not insulate that employer from liability."[39]

In a concurring opinion, written by Justice Thurgood Marshall, the concurring Justices found the question of employer liability "properly before us" and held that "sexual harassment by a supervisor of an employee under his supervision, leading to a discriminatory work environment, should be imputed to the employer for

Title VII purposes, regardless of whether the employee gave 'notice' of the offense."[40]

In so holding, the concurring opinion rejects the EEOC's position in *Meritor Savings Bank* as "untenable,"[41] and adopts the EEOC position initially set forth with its guidelines on sexual harassment in 1980.

> The Commission, in issuing the Guidelines, explained that its rule was "in keeping with the general standard of employer liability with respect to agents and supervisory employees . . . [T]he Commission and the courts have held for years that an employer is liable if a supervisor or an agent violates Title VII, regardless of knowledge or any other mitigating factor." 45 Fed. Reg. 74676 (1980).[42]

That standard is reasonable, the concurring opinion found, because "an employer can act only through individual supervisors and employees; discrimination is rarely carried out pursuant to a formal vote of a corporation's board of directors."[43] The concurring opinion also rejected the EEOC's suggestion in its brief to the Supreme Court in *Meritor Savings Bank* that a different rule should apply when a supervisor's harassment "merely" results in a discriminatory work environment. The concurring Justices countered:

> A supervisor's responsibilities do not begin and end with the power to hire and fire and discipline employees, or with the power to recommend such actions. Rather, a supervisor is charged with the day-to-day supervision of the work environment and with ensuring a safe, productive work place. There is no reason why abuse of the latter authority should have different consequences than abuse of the former.[44]

Moreover, the concurring opinion found

> No such requirement appears in the statute, and no such requirement can be coherently drawn from the law of agency.[45]

Since the U. S. Supreme Court's decision in *Meritor Savings Bank,* no lower court decision has followed the strict liability rule in the *Vinson v. Taylor* appellate court decision. All have harkened back to earlier cases to cite a no-strict liability rule for supervisors who create a hostile work environment. In *Delgado v. Lehman,*[46] where the plaintiff alleged that the manager of the employer's equal opportunity employment office created a hostile work environment, the court cited *Meritor Savings Bank* for the proposition that there was a cause of action for hostile work environment and *Katz v. Dole* at 709 F. 2d 256, for the liability rule that requires notice and corrective action by the employer.[47]

The *Delgado* court found that the employer was liable because it had actual notice and took no corrective action.[48]

However, as noted above, the results in *Delgado* and *Sapp* are not truly in accord with the *Henson* court decision that corrective action does not negate liability, but may mitigate damages.[49] In both cases, the courts do not reach the issue of employer liability. In *Scott,* the court cites cases on both sides of the question including the U.S. Supreme Court's discussion including the majority and concurring opinions in *Meritor Savings Bank.*[50] In *Rabidue,* the court cites only cases where there is no strict liability rule.[51]

In summary, the lower courts are split on employer liability when supervisors create a hostile work environment. The majority in the Supreme Court decision in *Meritor Savings Bank* declined to rule definitively on the issue, but hinted that strict liability may not be appropriate. The concurring opinion took the opposite view. No court decisions since *Meritor Savings Bank* offer any real guidance.

FOOTNOTES

[1] *Katz v. Dole,* 709 F.2d 251, 31 FEP Cases 1521, 1524 (4th Cir. 1983); *Vinson v. Taylor,* 23 FEP Cases 37 (D.D.C. 1980); *Ferguson v. duPont Co.,* 560 F. Supp. 1172, 31 FEP Cases 795 (D. Dela. 1983); *Henson v. City of Dundee,* 682 F. 2d 897, 29 FEP Cases 787 (11th Cir. 1982); *Coley v. Conrail,* 561 F.2d 645, 34 FEP Cases 129, 133 (E. D. Mich. 1982); *Davis v. Western-Southern Life Ins. Co.,* 34 FEP Cases 97 (N. D. Ohio, 1984).

[2] 682 F.2d 897, 29 FEP Cases 787, at 799.

[3] 560 F. Supp. 1172, 31 FEP Cases 795, at 814, citing *Henson,* 682 F.2d 897, 29 FEP Cases 787, at 798.

[4] *Id.* at 814.

[5] *Id.*

[6] *Id.* at 798 n. 19.

[7] *Bundy v. Jackson,* 641 F.2d 934, 24 FEP Cases 1155, 1162 (D. C. Cir. 1981);

Vinson v. Taylor, 753 F.2d 141, 36 FEP Cases 1423 (D.C. Cir. 1985); *Jeppsen v. Wunnicke,* 611 F. Supp. 78, 37 FEP Cases 994 (D. Alaska 1985); *Brown v. City of Guthrie,* 22 FEP Cases 1627, 1633 (W.D. Oklahoma 1980).

[8] 641 F.2d 934, 24 FEP Cases 1155,at 1162.

[9] 753 F.2d 141, 36 FEP Cases 1423, at 1428.

[10] *Id.* at 1431.

[11] *Id.* at 1430.

[12] *Id.*

[13] *Restatement (Second) of Agency,* Section 219(2)(1958) as cited in concurring opinion of Judge MacKinnon, in *Barnes v. Costle,* 561 F. 2d 983, 995, 15 FEP 345 (D.C. Cir. 1977).

See also *New EEOC Guidelines for Discrimination because of Sex: Employer Liability for Sexual Harassment Under Title VII,* 61 B. U. L. REV. 535, 539 (1981) cited in *Vinson,* 753 F.2d 141, 36 FEP Cases 1423, at 1431 n. 76. to read that under strict common law test, vicarious Title VII responsibility would be rare.

[14] *Id.* at 1431.

[15] *Id.*

[16] *Id.*

[17] *Id.*

[18] *Id.*

[19] *Id.*

[20] 611 F. Supp. 78, 37 FEP Cases 994 (D. Alaska 1985).

[21] *Id.* at 997.

[22] *Id.*

[23] *Id.*

[24] *Id.*

[25] *Id.*

[26] *Meritor Savings Bank v. Vinson,* — U.S. —, 106 S. Ct. 2399, 54 LW 4703, 40 FEP Cases 1822 (1986).

[27] *Vinson v. Taylor,* 23 FEP Cases 37 (D.D.C. 1980).

[28] *Vinson v. Taylor,* 753 F. 2d 141, 36 FEP Cases 1423 (D. C. Cir. 1985).

[29] — U.S. —,106 S. Ct. 2399 at 2408.

[30] *Id.*

[31] *Id.*

[32] 753 F.2d 141, 36 FEP Cases 1423, at 1431.

[33] — U.S. —, 106 S. Ct. 2399, at 2408.

[34] *Id.*

[35] *Id.*

[36] *Id.*

[37] 29 C.F.R. Section 1604.11(c).

[38] *Id.*

[39] — U.S. —, 106 S. Ct. 2399, at 2408.

[40] *Id.* at 2411.
[41] *Id.* at 2410.
[42] *Id.* at 2409–2410.
[43] *Id.* at 2410.
[44] *Id.*
[45] *Id.*
[46] 43 FEP Cases 593 (6th Cir. 1987).
[47] 43 FEP Cases at 599.
[48] *Id.* at 600.

See also *Sapp v. City of Warner Robins,* 43 FEP Cases 486, 491 (M.D. Georgia 1987), where court relying on no-strict liability rule in *Henson* 682 F.2d at 905, found notice and corrective action, hence, no employer liability.

[49] 682 F.2d 897, 29 FEP Cases 787, at 798 n. 19.

See also *Scott v. Sears, Roebuck & Co.,* 798 F.2d 210, 41 FEP Cases 805, 808 (7th Cir. 1986), *affirming,* 605 F. Supp. 1047, 37 FEP Cases 878 (N.D. Ill. 1985) and *Rabidue v. Osceola Refining Co.,* 42 FEP Cases 631 (6th Cir. 1986), *affirming,* 584 F. Supp. 419, 36 FEP Cases 183 (E.D. Mich. 1984).

[50] 798 F.2d 210, 41 FEP Cases 805, at 808, n. 3.
[51] e.g. *Barrett v. Omaha National Bank,* 726 F.2d 424, 427–28, 35 FEP Cases 593 (8th Cir. 1984); *Katz v. Dole,* 709 F.2d 251, 255–56, 31 FEP Cases 1521 (4th Cir. 1983); and *Henson v. City of Dundee,* 682 F.2d 897, 910 n. 20, 20 FEP Cases 787 (11th Cir. 1982). Both appellate court decisions are post-*Meritor.*

§3:07. —Cases Involving Co-Workers.

While supervisors can be implicated in both *quid quo pro* and hostile work environment cases, in the majority of cases involving co-workers, the sexual harassment takes the form of hostile work environment only, because co-workers do not have the power over a fellow employee to create a *quid pro quo* situation. *Scott v. Sears, Roebuck & Co.*[1]

The employer is liable for the actions of these employees under the EEOC guidelines "where the employer (or its agents or supervisory employees) knows or should have known of the conduct, unless it can be shown that it took immediate and appropriate corrective action."[2]

The courts have upheld this standard of liability and have found that the plaintiff's burden is to prove, according to the court in *Katz v. Dole,*[3] that "the complaints about the harassment were lodged with the employer or that the harassment was so pervasive that employer awareness may be inferred." In *Zabkowicz v. West Bend Co.,*[4] the court found that the "evidence abundantly demonstrates the defendant's knowledge of the harassment."

In *Scott v. Sears, Roebuck & Co.,*[5] the lower court found that the plaintiff cannot attribute to her employer either actual or constructive knowledge of the sexual harassment "where she admits she never complained to a superior and offers no evidence that her employer knew of the harassment by her co-workers."[6] In *Wimberly v. Shoney's Inc.,*[7] the court ruled that there was no credible evidence that any of the plaintiffs ever complained to higher management about sexual harassment. In addition, the courts did not find the acts so pervasive "so as to impute knowledge to (the employer)."[8] Likewise, in *Ukarish v. Magnesium Elektron,*[9] the court found that the plaintiff had not complained to higher management and she complained only once to a middle manager who "responded promptly." Moreover, the court found that the atmosphere complained of was not so pervasive to "give rise to an inference of knowledge or constructive knowledge." The court wrote:

> The general atmosphere of language in the plant was a fact of life which existed there long before Mrs. Ukarish arrived. It did not materially change during the course of her employment there, and there was no indications that she was so offended that there should be significant steps taken to materially alter that atmosphere.[10]

As to the showing required by the courts that the employer has taken corrective action, the court in *Katz v. Dole,*[11] articulated it as "prompt remedial action reasonably calculated to end the harassment." In *Zabkowicz v. West Bend Co.,*[12] the court held that the employer, with much notice ("five or six complaints about offensive language," "being handed three or four offensive drawings"), failed to take corrective action. "That it was within the defendants' capability to halt the harassment campaign is demonstrated by the events which occurred after Mrs. Zabkowicz filed her EEOC complaint."[13] Those actions included a three-day investigation which resulted in the discharge of one "tormentor" and suspension of three others. Then, the court found, "the nearly four years of harassment ceased immediately."[14]

In *Barrett v. Omaha National Bank,*[15] the plaintiff alleged that the employer's corrective action was inadequate. Plaintiff was a personal banker, who after attending a two-day conference with a co-worker, returned to work and complained to a vice-president that her co-worker had talked to her about "sexual activity and touched her in an offensive way."[16] Within four days of the complaint, an investigation resulted in the co-worker being reprimanded and told further misconduct of this nature would result in discharge. Plaintiff argued that her employer took "no action to ensure that her working environment was free from future hostility." The court disagreed, finding "ample evidence" that the employer had taken "immediate and appropriate corrective action,"[17] and held that the employer had not violated Title VII.

FOOTNOTES

[1] 605 F. Supp 1047, 37 FEP Cases 878 (N. D. Ill, 1985), *affirmed* 798 F.2d 210, 41 FEP 805 (7th Cir. 1986); *Barrett v. Omaha National Bank,* 726 F.2d 424, 35 FEP Cases 593 (8th Cir. 1984); *Wimberly v. Shoney's Inc.,* 39 FEP Cases 444 (S. D. Georgia 1985); *Zabkowicz v. West Bend Co.,* 589 F. Supp. 780, 35 FEP Cases 611 (E. D. Wisc, 1984); *Ukarish v. Magnesium Elektron,* 31 FEP Cases 1315 (D. N.J. 1983); *Martin v. Norbar, Inc.,* 537 F. Supp. 1260, 30 FEP Cases 103, 104 (S. D. Ohio, 1982).

But see *contra, Robson v. Eva's Supermarket,* 30 FEP Cases 1212, 1217 (N. D. Ohio, 1982) where the co-worker with some supervisory functions could be held to standards of supervisor.

See also *Continental Can v. State of Minnesota,* 22 FEP Cases 1808 (Minn. Supreme Ct. 1980), which was prior to *Bundy* but after EEOC guidelines on sexual harassment were issued. Court found cause of action for hostile work environment and employer liability based on notice and corrective action.

[2] 29 C.F.R. Section 1604.11(d).

[3] 709 F.2d 251, 31 FEP Cases 1521, 1524 (4th Cir. 1983).

[4] 589 F. Supp. 780, 35 FEP Cases 610, 613 (E.D. Wisc. 1984).

[5] 605 F. Supp. 1047, 36 FEP Cases 878 (N. D. Ill. 1985), *affirmed* 798 F.2d 210, 41 FEP Cases 805 (7th Cir. 1986).

[6] *Id.* at 883.
[7] 39 FEP Cases 444 (S. D. Georgia 1985).
[8] *Id.* at 453.
[9] 31 FEP Cases 1315, 1322 (D. N.J. 1983).
[10] *Id.*
[11] 709 F.2d 251, 31 FEP Cases 1521, 1524 (4th Cir. 1983).
[12] 589 F. Supp. 780, 35 FEP Cases 611 (E. D. Wisc. 1984).
[13] *Id. at 613.*
[14] *Id.*
[15] 726 F.2d 424, 35 FEP Cases 593 (8th Cir. 1984).
[16] *Id.* at 594.
[17] *Id.*

§3:08. Individual Liability for Sexual Harassment.

Some courts have found that, although *respondeat superior* makes an employer liable for the acts of its supervisors and agents, it is sometimes appropriate for employees themselves to be individually liable for the discriminatory acts they have committed. This individual liability is not found often but is warranted "[W]hen a party's deliberate conduct is so extreme that it intentionally interferes with another's ability to practice a profession or earn a livelihood."[1] There the court found that the co-workers made the plaintiff's work environment "intolerable."[2]

> They shot rubber bands at her. They engaged in boisterous speculation about her virginity. They circulated an obscene cartoon depiction of her.[3]

However in *Hendrix v. Fleming Cos.,*[4] the court ruled that an employee who made "rude remarks and sexual advances" toward the plaintiff might be individually liable for his behavior, but not other individual defendants, who were employees who "allegedly either knew or should have known about (the) . . . conduct and did nothing to stop it."[5] Thus, the court concluded, "it appears that actual misfeasance, as opposed to non-feascence, is necessary for individual liability under Title VII."[6]

FOOTNOTES

[1] *Kyriazi v. Western Electric Co.*, 176 F. Supp. 335, 26 FEP Cases 413 (D. N.J. 1979).
[2] *Id.* at 417.
[3] *Id.*
[4] 650 F. Supp 301, 42 FEP Cases 461, 462 (W. D. Oklahoma 1986).
[5] *Id.*
[6] *Id.*

§3:09. Liability of Non Employees for Sexual Harassment.

Beyond an employer's liability for the acts of co-workers who create a hostile work environment, the courts have also extended liability to offensive conduct by an independent contractor in *State of N.Y. v. Hamilton,*[1] where an independent polygraph examiner was involved and to offensive conduct by customers. The EEOC guidelines on sexual harassment specifically address the liability of an employer for the acts of non-employees.

> An employer may also be responsible for the acts of non-employees . . . where the employer (or its agents or supervisory employees) knows or should have known of the conduct and fails to take immediate and appropriate corrective action. In reviewing these cases, the Commission will consider the extent of the employer's control and any other legal responsibility which the employer may have with respect to the conduct of such employees.[2]

These guidelines were adopted in light of *EEOC v. Sage Realty Corp.*[3] There the court held that the employer was liable for the conduct of customers and members of the public who sexually harassed plaintiff in her job as lobby receptionist. The court found that the harassment was "a result of the employer's requirement that the plaintiff wear a uniform that was "revealing and sexually provocative."[4]

The court outlined the evidence present in the case by which plaintiff established her *prima facie* case:

> There is no question that defendants . . . required (the plaintiff) to wear the . . . uniform because she was a woman. Due to its revealing

> nature, the uniform caused (the plaintiff) to endure harassment in the performance of her job. The wearing of the uniform was made a condition of (her) employment and her employment was terminated when she refused to continue wearing the garment.[5]

Two important facts emerge in the court's ruling in *EEOC v. Sage Realty Corp.* One is that the plaintiff made numerous complaints about the uniform and its revealing nature to her employer before and after she wore it on the job. The court recounted the facts.

> When (the plaintiff) tried on her uniform, she found it short and revealing on both sides. Her thighs and portions of her buttocks were exposed, and understandably she was concerned about wearing the outfit in the. . . . lobby.[6]

The plaintiff complained about the uniform to her employer and had it altered before she wore it on the job, even though she believed that the alterations were inadequate. After two days of wear, the court found that she "received a number of sexual propositions and endured lewd comments and gestures. Humiliated by what occurred, (the plaintiff) was unable to perform her duties properly."[7]

The plaintiff refused to wear the uniform again on the job and complained both verbally and in writing to her immediate supervisors and their superiors about the uniform and the harassment. In response, the president of the company gave her the "choice of either wearing the uniform or leaving the floor."[8] This ultimately led to her discharge.

The second significant fact in *EEOC v. Sage Realty Corp.,* was that the employer had the ability to control the conduct of non-employees toward the plaintiff, by either significantly altering the uniform or not requiring the plaintiff to wear it on the job. The employer did neither and was held liable by the court under Title VII.[9]

The absence of one of these two facts was the determining factor in a subsequent EEOC decision, regarding three female employees of a women's clothing store who alleged that they were required to wear a swimsuit outfit which was "sexually revealing." Wearing that outfit, they claimed, would have subjected them to "embarrassment and offensive remarks and conduct."[10]

The EEOC ruled, that although there was precedent in both the EEOC guidelines on sexual harassment and in case law for their case, the women had no proof that if they wore the costume, they would have been sexually harassed. Because they were discharged by the employer for refusing to wear the outfit in the first place, they failed to establish employer liability for the sexual harassment that might have happened.

FOOTNOTES

[1] N. Y. Sup. Ct., No. H49547, August 20, 1985.

[2] C.F.R. Section 1604.11(e).

[3] 507 F. Supp. 599, 24 FEP Cases 1521 (S.D.N.Y. 1981).

See also *EEOC v. Sage Realty Corp.,* 87 F.R.D. 365, 22 FEP Cases 1660 (S.D.N.Y. 1980) where defendant's motion for summary judgment was denied.

[4] 507 F. Supp. 599, 24 FEP Cases 1521, at 1528.

See in accord on a cause of action under Title VII for actions of non-employees, *Marentette v. Michigan Host, Inc.,* 506 F. Supp. 909, 24 FEP Cases 1665 (E. D. 1980).

[5] 507 F. Supp. 599, 24 FEP Cases 1521.

[6] *Id. at 1526.*

[7] *Id.*

[8] *Id. at 1527.*

[9] *Id.*

[10] *Id.*

§3:10. Summary.

Thus, as a result of the 1980 guidelines on sexual harassment issued by the federal Equal Employment Opportunity Commission (EEOC) and the decisions of courts in the area of sexual harassment, there has evolved a set of rules governing the extent of an employer's liability regarding sexual harassment of employees. Some of those rules are quite settled, such as an employer is strictly liable for the acts of supervisors in *quid pro quo* sexual harassment cases. Others are yet to be definitely decided, most notably whether an employer is strictly liable for acts of supervisors that create a hostile work environment. This evolutionary process will continue as the courts continue to decide sexual harassment cases under Title VII and formulate rules of liability for employers.

CHAPTER FOUR

An Employer's Defenses to Sexual Harassment

§4:01. Overview.

After the plaintiff has established a *prima facie* case of employment discrimination, the burden of production of evidence in a Title VII case shifts to the employer to articulate some legitimate, non-discriminatory reason for the actions it took. The employer must produce evidence that the employee was fired, not promoted, demoted or lost some other job benefit for a reason other than discrimination on the basis of a classification (e.g. race, sex, national origin) protected by Title VII.

This shifting of the burden of production to the employer is the second step of a three-step analysis employed by the courts in Title VII cases. This process was first set forth in *McDonnell Douglas Corp. v. Green,*[1] and *Texas Department of Community Affairs v. Burdine,*[2] and was more fully articulated in *United States Postal Service Board of Governors v. Aikens.*[3]

The third step in the analysis gives the plaintiff the opportunity to prove that the reasons offered by the employer were not the true ones, but merely a pretext for discrimination. This pretext can be "that a discriminatory reason more likely motivated the employer."[4]

This chapter will explore the second and third step of this

analysis as it has been applied in sexual harassment cases. Not every court decision in a sexual harassment case will reach these steps in the analysis, however, because many plaintiffs fail to establish a *prima facie* case of discrimination, under the first step of this analysis. That is, the plaintiff does not alleged or prove sufficient facts to constitute illegal sexual harassment. (See discussion of the plaintiff's *prima facie* case earlier in this book.)

The cases examined below are those in which the court, upon being persuaded by the plaintiff that some form of sexual harassment has occurred, then examines the employer's evidence to find a legitimate business reason, beside the sexual harassment, that actions were taken against the employee.

This chapter will also look at other defenses that can be raised by an employer in a sexual harassment Title VII case including the existence of a company policy against sexual harassment.

FOOTNOTES

[1] 411 U.S. 792, 5 FEP Cases 965 (1973).
[2] 450 U.S. 248, 25 FEP Cases 113 (1981).
[3] 460 U.S. 711, 31 FEP Cases 609 (1983).
[4] 450 U.S. 248 at 256, 25 FEP Cases 113 (1981).

§4:02. Legitimate Business Reasons for Actions Against an Employee.

An employer can give many different reasons for taking an adverse action against an employee. In sexual harassment cases, the courts have examined a variety of reasons.

§4:03. —Excessive Absenteeism or Tardiness.

1) *Ambrose v. U.S. Steel Corp.,*[1]—Plaintiff was discharged for excessive absenteeism which the court found was pretextual.

2) *Meyers v. I.T.T. Diversified Credit Corp.,*[2]—Plaintiff was discharged for excessive absenteeism and disregard of duties which the court ruled pretextual.

3) *Sand v. Johnson Co.*,[3]—Plaintiff was properly discharged for "habitual tardiness."

4) *Craig v. Y & Y Snacks, Inc.*,[4]—Plaintiff was terminated for her unacceptable absenteeism and tardiness record, a reason which the court found pretextual.

Footnotes

[1] 39 FEP Cases 30 (N.D. Calif. 1985).
[2] 527 F. Supp. 1064, 27 FEP Cases 995 (E. D. Mo. 1981).
[3] 33 FEP Cases 717 (E. D. Mich. 1982).
[4] 721 F.2d 77, 33 FEP Cases 187 (3rd. Cir. 1983).

§4:04. —Poor Performance.

1) *Bouchet v. National Urban League,*[1]—Plaintiff was properly terminated because she lacked necessary experience and qualifications to meet demands of job.

2) *Burns v. Terre Haute Regional H½osp.*,[2]—Plaintiff was properly discharged for poor attitude toward her job and employer.

3) *Mays v. Williamson & Sons,*[3]—Plaintiff was terminated for poor job performance and excessive tardiness and absenteeism which the court found pretextual.

4) *Rabidue v. Osceola Refining Co.*,[4]—Plaintiff was properly discharged because she was "willful, rude and inclined not to follow employer's policies."

5) *Robinson v. duPont Co.*,[5]—Plaintiff was properly denied promotion and transferred and ultimately discharged for failure to improve "personality problems" she had which affected her job performance.

6) *EEOC v. Domino's Pizza, Inc.*,[6]—Plaintiff was not discharged for any business reason, legitimate or not, where she was discharged "as a primary and direct result" of her refusal to submit to her supervisor's sexual advances after she was the

"victim of a unsolicited, unwanted and offensive" physical sexual assault by him.[7]

7) *Phillips v. Smalley Maintenance Services,*[8]—Plaintiff was discharged for poor work performance but court found reason pretextual.

8) *Heelan v. Johns-Manville Corp.,*[9]—Plaintiff was terminated for poor job performance which court found was pretextual.

9) *Hall v. F. O. Thacker Co.,*[10]—Plaintiff properly discharged for failing to meet "minimum requirements" of secretarial job.

10) *Harrison v. Reed Rubber Co.,*[11]—Plaintiff was demoted from her job as foreman for poor job performance, which court found pretextual.

11) *Williams v. Civiletti,*[12]—Plaintiff was discharged for poor work performance, which the court found pretextual.

12) *Hill v. BASF Wyandotte, Corp.,*[13]—Plaintiff was properly discharged for poor attitude and failing to perform her work.

13) *Lamb v. Drilco Div.,*[14]—Plaintiff was terminated for "poor performance" which the court found pretextual because her decline in job performance was due to the existence of unlawful sexual harassment in the workplace.

14) *Evans v. Mail Handlers Union,*[15]—Plaintiff was properly demoted and subsequently discharged when her job was abolished in a company reorganization. The employer found that the work relationship had deteriorated between the plaintiff and her supervisor because of a consensual sexual relationship, and they "had to be separated."

FOOTNOTES

[1] 33 FEP Cases 535 (D.D.C. 1982).

[2] 581 F. Supp. 1301, 37 FEP Cases 1304 (S. D. Ill. 1983).

[3] 591 F. Supp. 1518, 35 FEP Cases 1869, (E. D. Arkansas 1984), *affirmed,* 775 F.2d 258, 39 FEP Cases 106 (8th Cir. 1985).

[4] 584 F. Supp. 419, 36 FEP Cases 183 (E. D. Mich. 1984), *affirmed,* 805 F. 2d 611, 42 FEP Cases 631 (6th Cir. 1986).
[5] 33 FEP Cases 880 (D. Delaware 1979).
[6] 34 FEP Cases 1075 (E.D. Mich. 1983).
[7] *Id.* at 1076.
[8] 711 F.2d 1524, 32 FEP Cases 975 (11th Cir. 1983).
[9] 451 F. Supp. 1382, 20 FEP Cases 251 (D. Colo. 1978).
[10] 24 FEP Cases 1499 (N.D. Georgia 1980).
[11] 603 F. Supp. 1457, 37 FEP Cases 1545 (E. D. Mo. 1985).
[12] 487 F. Supp. 1387, 22 FEP Cases 1311 (D.D.C. 1980), *on remand,* 17 FEP Cases 1662 (D.C. Cir. 1978).
[13] 27 FEP 66 (E. D. Mich. 1981).
[14] 32 FEP Cases 105 (S. D. Texas 1983).
[15] 32 FEP Cases 634 (D.D.C. 1983).

§4:05. —Pretext.

The employer's burden in the second step of the analysis is merely to produce evidence, not proof, of its non-discriminatory motive. *Rabidue v. Osceola Refining Co.*[1] It is for the plaintiff, in the next step of the analysis, to prove by the preponderance of the evidence that "more likely than not, the asserted reasons for the employment decision are pretextual."[2]

Thus, plaintiff must persuade the court with clear evidence of pretext. In *Horn v. Duke Homes,*[3] this proof was in "thin" and "belated" complaints about the plaintiff's performance.[4] In *Williams v. Civiletti,*[5] the court found the requisite proof of pretext in the timing of criticism of plaintiff's work which began "only after (she) . . . rejected her supervisor's advances." The court ruled that "her rejections of the advances spawned the criticism of her work and eventually led to her dismissal."[6]

The court found proof of pretext in *Craig v. Y & Y Snacks, Inc.,*[7] in plaintiff's testimony that she was not suspended for three days as a warning prior to discharge as required in the employer's personnel policies.[8] The employer argued that it had suspended her but could not produce a record at trial. This evidence (or lack of it) led the district court to conclude that the plaintiff was terminated by her supervisor, not for "excessive absenteeism and tardiness," but "to get even" with her for rejecting his sexual advances. The appellate court upheld that finding and ruled that the employer had discharged plaintiff in violation of Title VII.[9]

The district court in *Mays v. Williamson & Sons Janitorial Services Inc.,*[10] found pretext when plaintiff testified that she had no knowledge of most of the memoranda placed in her personnel file regarding her poor work performance. She "disputed the integrity" of several memoranda that she supposedly made to herself and other documents written by the supervisor who was sexually harassing her.[11] The court concluded that "it is a highly suspect practice to place allegations of misconduct or poor work performance in an employee's personnel file without notice to the employee."[12] This finding of pretext was upheld on appeal.

In *Meyers v. I.T.T. Diversified Credit Corp.,*[13] where the plaintiff was allegedly fired for excessive absenteeism and poor job performance, the court was persuaded by the fact that the plaintiff had received a good job review and a merit raise seven months prior to her termination. Her time sheets also showed no absenteeism problem and her immediate supervisor said she was a good worker.[14] The court also noted that an employee with less experience was advanced over her and that procedures were instituted requiring her to submit a written report every time she wished to leave her post.[15] These facts proved pretext, the court concluded.

In *Phillips v. Smalley Maintenance Services,*[16] proof of pretext was found in the fact that the employer hired others soon after the plaintiff was terminated for positions she was qualified to fill or for which she had indicated an interest.[17]

In looking for proof of pretext in *Lamb v. Drilco*[18] the court examined the employer's explanation of the decline of plaintiff's work performance and noted the physical and mental state of the plaintiff that resulted from the "undisputed sexual harassment" she had encountered on her job. The court wrote:

> She was upset and unable to concentrate. She was unable to eat or sleep and eventually began to drink alcohol more than usual.[19]

From this examination, the court concluded that the reason for the discharge was "not legitimate because the Defendant employer created the problem initially."[26]

Similarly in *Harrison v. Reed Rubber Co.,*[21] the court gleaned pretext when it found that the company president was first aware of the harassment "just days before he relieved the plaintiff of her position as foreman, yet demoted her without considering the possible effect of the harassment on her performance."[22] Furthermore, the employer's only "credible" evidence of poor job performance was that the plaintiff was responsible for one error, which led the court to believe that her complaints of sexual harassment by her supervisor, a twenty year employee with the company, "were . . . in part responsible for her demotion."[23]

Other courts have found "no pretext" when the following proof was offered by the plaintiff. In *Burns v. Terre Haute Regional Hosp.,*[24] the acts of sexual harassment were "too attentuated" from the ultimate dismissal and other "reasonable grounds" were given for the discharge including the employer's "economic" situation and "concerns about plaintiff's attitude toward her job, her subordinates and her employers."[25]

In *Bouchet v. National Urban League,*[26] the employer produced evidence of letters of reprimand given to the plaintiff prior to discharge as well as of meetings in which plaintiff was told of her performance deficiencies.[27] While the court found the plaintiff "intelligent and capable," there was no proof that she possessed the "experience and competence to fulfill the legitimate demands placed on her."[28]

The plaintiff conceded at trial in *Robinson v. duPont Co.,*[29] a number of incidents of poor job performance, rudeness and warnings to improve her interpersonal behavior prior to her discharge.[30] The court ruled that she was denied a promotion and a transfer and finally terminated due to her "inability to improve certain personality problems she had and which adversely affected her working relationship with others."[31]

In *Hall v. F. O. Thacker Co.,*[32] the court credited the testimony of two employees who provided "ample proof" that plaintiff, a secretary, was frequently absent from job and had inadequate secretarial skills.[33] This substantiated employer's reason that the plaintiff was fired for not having the "minimum" qualifications for secretarial work.[34]

Some recent court decisions have coupled evidence of poor work performance with the failure of the plaintiff to allege a *prima facie* case of sexual harassment, that is, the acts were insufficient to constitute sexual harassment. For example, in *Neville v. Taft Broadcasting,*[35] the in-house company investigator concluded that the plaintiff had raised the sexual harassment complaint because "she wanted to save her job."[36] While the court did not infer that motive, it found no violation of Title VII where there was ample proof of "errors, poor servicing of accounts and complaints by clients,"[37] and only one alleged incident of sexual conduct by her supervisor.[38] In *Freedman v. American Standard,*[39] the court found plaintiff, a co-pilot, was discharged because of

> her failure to pass *three times* the basic flight checks on which her employment depended. Her failure to perform properly on any flight would obviously lead to loss of life and property. After failing twice, she negotiated a third test, where she practically dictated her own terms and, having put her position on the line with this flight check, did not only perform improperly, but displayed conduct that could only produce a disaster in the normal course of flying passengers.[40]

By this treatment, the employer, the court noted, "not only displayed concern for her instruction and advancement but gave her extraordinary consideration when a male pilot would have (and had) been discharged for failing one flight test."[41]

This evidence of poor job performance was persuasive in light of the fact that the only acts of sexual harassment proven were "an obscene message sent on one occasion, rudeness without a disclosed reason, an assignment once of a menial task or an accepted refusal of a date." These acts, the court held, did not "equate" to sexual harassment which created a hostile environment.[42]

Another court examined the nature of the interaction between two employees involved in "intermittent sexual relationships" to determine if the employer's reason for demoting and subsequently terminating the plaintiff was pretextual. In *Evans v. Mail Handlers Union,*[43] the court found "an astounding number of open sexual liaisons among Defendant's employees,"[44] including one between the plaintiff, a secretary and her immediate supervisor. The relationship began at the supervisor's initiation but was, the court concluded, "intermittent" and "completely consensual in nature."[45] When the plaintiff finally complained about her supervisor's actions, the personnel director met with both of them, "heard their respective complaints against each other" and decided that, since their work relationship had "soured," the "only solution" was to "separate the two." The plaintiff was offered and accepted a lower-paying position. Later, the plaintiff was terminated when her job was abolished in an office reorganization.[46]

In its decision, the court credited the testimony of the employer that the parties needed to be separated and that "their personal squabble was beginning to affect their work and their working relationship." That need, and no allegation of plaintiff's resistance to sexual advances, was the reason for the adverse actions taken, the court held.

Thus, the courts have examined the plaintiff's proof that the business reason given by the employer was pretextual with an eye to credibility and common sense. Courts have looked for instances where the complaints are "thin" and "belated" to find pretext and situations in which the plaintiff's job performance was very weak or below minimal standards to affirm that the business reason given by the employer was legitimate.

FOOTNOTES

[1] 584 F. Supp. 419, 36 FEP Cases 183, 187 (E.D. Mich. 1984).

[2] *Id.*

[3] 775 F.2d 599, 37 FEP Cases 230 (7th Cir. 1985).

[4] *Id.* at 230.

[5] 487 F. Supp. 1387, 22 FEP Cases 1311 (D.D.C. 1980), *on remand,* 17 FEP Cases 1662 (D.C. Cir. 1978).

[6] *Id.* at 1312.
[7] 721 F.2d 77, 33 FEP Cases 187 (3rd. Cir. 1983).
[8] *Id.* at 189.
[9] *Id.*
[10] 591 F. Supp. 1518, 35 FEP Cases 1868 (E.D. Ark. 1984), *affirmed,* 775 F.2d 258, 39 FEP Cases 106 (8th Cir. 1985).
[11] 591 F. Supp. 1518, 35 FEP Cases 1868, at 1871.
[12] *Id.*
[13] 527 F. Supp. 1064, 27 FEP Cases 995 (E. D. Mo. 1981).
[14] *Id.* at 997.
[15] *Id.* at 999.
[16] 711 F.2d 1524, 32 FEP Cases 975 (11th Cir. 1983).
[17] *Id.* at 978.
[18] 32 FEP Cases 105 (S. D. Texas, 1983).
[19] *Id.* at 106.
[20] *Id.* at 107.
[21] 603 F. Supp. 457, 37 FEP Cases 1545 (E.D. Mo. 1985).
[22] *Id.* at 1549.
[23] *Id.*
[24] 581 F. Supp. 1301, 37 FEP Cases 1304, 1309 (S.D. Ind. 1983).
[25] *Id.*
[26] 33 FEP Cases 535 (D.D.C. 1982).
[27] *Id.* at 539.
[28] *Id.* at 540.
[29] 33 FEP Cases 880 (D. Delaware 1979).
[30] *Id.* at 882.
[31] *Id.* at 883.
[32] 24 FEP Cases 1499 (N.D. Ga. 1980).
[33] *Id.* at 1503–1504.
[34] *Id.* at 1502.
[35] 42 FEP Cases 1314 (W.D.N.Y. 1987).
[36] *Id.* at 1323.
[37] *Id.* at 1323.
[38] *Id.* at 1317.
[39] 41 FEP Cases 471 (D. N.J. 1986).
[40] *Id.* at 476.
[41] *Id.*
[42] *Id.*
[43] 32 FEP Cases 634 (D.D.C. 1983).
[44] *Id.* at 635.
[45] *Id.*
[46] *Id.* at 636.

§4:06. The Existence of an Internal Grievance Procedure.

While the courts have been concerned with enforcing Title VII in specific cases of sexual harassment before them, they have also shown a genuine interest in having employers work to prevent sexual harassment in the workplace. Several courts have observed that employers can prevent sexual harassment by establishing internal grievance procedures for sexual harassment complaints and company policies that clearly articulate that such conduct is not acceptable in their workplace. In *Bundy v. Jackson,*[1] the appellate court noted that the prevention of sexual harassment was the major goal of the 1980 guidelines on sexual harassment issued by the Equal Employment Opportunity Commission (EEOC). The court wrote: "An employer should fashion rules within its firm or agency to ensure that . . . corrective action never becomes necessary."[2] It encouraged the district court to fashion a remedy on remand that required the employer to establish and publicize "a scheme whereby harassed employees may complain to the Director immediately and confidentially."[3] The court explained:

> The Director should promptly take all necessary steps to investigate and correct any harassment, including warnings and appropriate discipline directed at the offending party, and should generally develop other means of preventing harassment within the agency.[4]

Yet, while this goal of prevention is important, the question arises whether the existence of an employer-initiated internal grievance procedure is a defense to a sexual harassment case, especially when the employee does not use that procedure prior to filing a lawsuit. The courts have answered that question in two ways.

One court, *Miller v. Bank of America,*[5] found that an employer was not liable when it had a policy against sexual harassment and the plaintiff did not use it. The court wrote

> Where, as here, . . . there exists a company-wide policy expressly condemning the alleged misconduct and there exist responsive internal mechanisms established to process employee complaints of the in-

> stant sort, a failure on the part of the employee allegedly aggrieved by the condemned practice to avail . . . herself of these internal avenues of redress renders tenuous a finding of employer culpability.[6]

The court added:

> The Court is not to be understood as holding that exhaustion of company remedies is a prerequisite to suit under Title VII. Rather, a failure of exhaustion goes more to whether the employer is liable at all. (Citation omitted.)[7]

On appeal, the Ninth Circuit Court of Appeals disagreed and wrote: "We decline to read an exhaustion of company remedies requirement into Title VII."[8] This court relied on the U. S. Supreme Court decision in *McDonnell Douglas Corp. v. Green,*[9] where it was found that Title VII does not "restrict a complainant's right to sue."[10] It relied also on established Title VII case law that an employee need not exhaust union remedies as a prerequisite to a Title VII suit. The U.S. Supreme Court wrote in *Alexander v. Gardner-Denver Co.,*[11] "[a]n employee's Title VII rights are independent of contractual rights."

Subsequent court decisions again raised the issue. In *Vinson v. Taylor,*[12] the district court found that the plaintiff had never complained to her employer about the acts of sexual harassment by her supervisor and she had never filed a grievance regarding this conduct through the established in-house grievance procedure. Furthermore, the district court noted that the bank had a policy asserting its "dedication to equal treatment and employee rights." Therefore, the bank, without notice of the sexual harassment, was not liable for it.[13]

On appeal, the Circuit Court of Appeals for the District of Columbia,[14] reversed that finding of employer liability and observed:

> The bare existence of a company policy of nondiscrimination does not affect the employer's chargeability. . . . but it affords small comfort when violations go unrectified.[15]

In *Meritor Savings Bank v. Vinson,*[16] which was the appeal to the U. S. Supreme Court of the *Vinson v. Taylor* case, the parties and the EEOC, as *amicus curiae,* had different views of the plaintiff's need to use an internal grievance procedure. The plaintiff argued that she did not need to use the employer's grievance procedure, "because notice to (the supervisor who was harassing the plaintiff) was notice to the bank." She urged the Court to hold the supervisor to a rule of strict liability for supervisor's acts of sexual harassment.[17] (See previous chapters for a discussion of *respondeat superior* in sexual harassment cases.)

The employer contended that the plaintiff's failure to use its procedure "insulates" it from liability for the wrongdoing of its supervisor. The employer added, "a contrary rule would be unfair."[18]

The EEOC in its brief as *amicus curiae* argued

> If the employer had an expressed policy against sexual harassment and has implemented a procedure specifically designed to resolve sexual harassment claims, and if the victim does not take advantage of that procedure, the employer should be shielded from liability. . . .[19]

The EEOC added:

> In all other cases, the employer will be liable if it has actual knowledge of the harassment or if, considering all the facts of the case, the victim in question had no reasonably available avenue for making his or her complaints known to appropriate management officials.[20]

The Supreme Court responded by declining "the parties' invitation to set forth a definite rule" of when an employee must give notice to an employer when a supervisor creates a hostile work environment.[21] However, the Court did reject the employers' view that "the mere existence of a grievance procedure and a policy against discrimination coupled with (the plaintiff's) failure to invoke that procedure, must insulate (the employer) from liability."[22] The Court also indicated two major problems with the bank's policy and procedure.

First, the employer's general non-discrimination policy did not address sexual harassment in particular and "thus did not alert employees to their employer's interest in correcting that form of discrimination."[23]

Secondly, the bank's grievance procedure apparently required an employee to complain first to her supervisor. But since Vinson's supervisor was, in fact, the alleged perpetrator, "it is not altogether surprising that (the plaintiff) failed to invoke the procedure and report her grievance to him."[24]

The Court concluded:

> (The employer's) contention that (the plaintiff's) failure should insulate it from liability might be substantially stronger if its procedure were better calculated to encourage victims of harassment to come forward.[25]

Thus, while the Supreme Court in *Meritor Savings Bank* did not state that an employer policy and procedure are a complete defense to sexual harassment, the decision does suggest that an employer should adopt a policy against sexual harassment and company procedure for sexual harassment complaints. Two key elements of that policy and procedure, according to the Supreme Court, are that the policy be specific sexual harassment complaints and the procedure provide an employee with several avenues of complaint aside from an immediate supervisor, who may in fact be the harasser. It is also clear as the court stated in *Katz v. Dole,*[26] that an employer must do more than merely "indicate the existence of an official policy against (sexual) harassment."[27]

FOOTNOTES

[1] 641 F.2d 934, 24 FEP Cases 1155 (D.C. Cir. 1982).
[2] *Id.* at 1163.
[3] *Id.*
[4] *Id.*
[5] 418 F. Supp. 233, 13 FEP Cases 439 (N.D. Calif. 1976).
[6] *Id.* at 236.
[7] *Id.*
[8] 600 F.2d 211, 20 FEP Cases 462, 464 (9th Cir. 1979).

[9] 411 U.S. 792, 93 S.Ct. 1817, 36 L. Ed.2d 668, 5 FEP Cases (1981).

[10] *Id.* at 798.

[11] 415 U.S. 36, 49–50, 94 S. Ct. 1011, 39 L.Ed.2d 147, 7 FEP Cases 81, 87 (1974).

[12] 23 FEP Cases 37 (D.D.C. 1980).

[13] *Id.* at 42.

[14] 753 F.2d 141, 36 FEP Cases 1423 (D.C. Cir. 1985).

[15] *Id.* at 1430, n. 71.

See also *Cummings v. Walsh Construction Co.*, 561 F. Supp. 872, 31 FEP Cases 930, 933 (S.D. Ga. 1983).

[16] —— U.S. ——, 106 S. Ct. 2399, 40 FEP Cases 1822 (1986).

[17] *Id.* at 2407.

[18] *Id.*

[19] *Id.* at 2408.

[20] *Id.*

[21] *Id.* at 2408.

[22] *Id.* at 2408–2409.

[23] *Id.* at 2409.

[24] *Id.*

[25] *Id.*

[26] 709 F.2d 251, 31 FEP Cases 1521 (4th Cir. 1983).

[27] *Id.* at 600.

§4:07. Retaliation Against Employees for Filing a Complaint.

What else needs to be included in an in-house company policy against sexual harassment and a procedure for complaints can be gleaned from other court decisions. One element identified is that a complainant will not be retailiated against for making a complaint.

This is essential, first of all, because the courts have recognized that employees will be reticent to complain about sexual harassment. In *Jeppsen v. Wunnicke,*[1] the court indicated a concern for the employee being sexually harassed who is most dependent financially on her job. She "is likely to be the one most reticent to complain, and thereby pass knowledge to a higher supervisor" because she might find that "her complaint is not taken seriously, poor performance ratings start appearing and ultimately a promotion . . . denied."[2]

Secondly, retaliation is a separate cause of action under Title VII,[3] which prohibits an employer from taking any action against an employee because he has opposed any practice made illegal under Title VII or has filed a charge or participated in any way in a Title VII investigation or proceeding. The courts in sexual harassment case, and indeed for all complaints of employment discrimination under Title VII have recognized this separate cause of action for retaliation.[4]

FOOTNOTES

[1] 611 F. Supp. 78, 37 FEP Cases 994, 997 (D. Alaska 1985).

[2] *Id.*

[3] 42 U.S.C. Section 2000e-3(a).

[4] *Ludington v. Sambo's Restaurants Inc.*, 474 F. Supp. 480, 20 FEP Cases 1000 (E. D. Wisc 1979); *Sand v. Johnson,* 33 FEP Cases 716, 719 (E. D. Mich. 1982); *Mays v. Williamson & Sons Janitorial Services, Inc.*, 591 F. Supp 1518, 35 FEP Cases 1868, 1870 (E. D. Ark. 1984), *affirmed,* 775 F.2d 258, 39 FEP Cases 106 (8th Cir. 1985); *Barrett v. Omaha National Bank,* 584 F. Supp. 22, 35 FEP Cases 585 (D. Neb. 1983), *affirmed,* 726 F.2d 424, 35 FEP Cases 593, 595 (8th Cir. 1984); *Evans v. Mail Handlers Union,* 32 FEP Cases 634 (D.D.C. 1983); *Cobb v. DuFresne-Henry Inc.*, 603 F. Supp. 1048, 37 FEP Cases 1287 (D. Vt. 1985); *Jones v. Lyng,* 42 FEP Cases 587 (D.D.C. 1986).

§4:08. —Employer's Remedial Action.

Another critical element in a grievance procedure is that the employer will take prompt, immediate corrective action upon receiving a complaint of sexual harassment. Employers who have failed to take such action in a sexual harassment case have been most vulnerable to litigation and to liability in court.[1]

In *Katz v. Dole,* the appellate court found

> The record is devoid of significant evidence to contradict Katz' claim that her employment by the FAA was conditioned by a pattern of personally directed sexual insult and innuendo. Furthermore, despite their knowledge of this harassment, her employer's supervisory personnel did nothing effectual to stop, and indeed, in (one supervisor's) case, took part in it.[2]

In *Bundy v. Jackson,*[3] the court found that when Bundy complained about the sexual advances to the superior of the two supervisors who were harassing her, that superior "casually dismissed Bundy complaints, telling her that 'any man in his right mind would want to rape you' and then proceeded "himself to request that she begin a sexual relationship with him in his apartment."[4]

Here, the court held that the employer had "full notice of harassment committed by agency supervisors and did virtually nothing to stop or even investigate the practice."[5] The supervisors' failure to act indicated to the court that sexual advances by males in this office to female employees was "considered a game that was played and not to be taken seriously."[6]

On the other hand, an employer can act quickly and effectively to stop the sexual harassment. In *Zabkowicz v. West Bend Co.,*[7] the results of a three day investigation resulted in one of the harassers being fired and three others suspended. The harassment, which had lasted for four years, immediately stopped.

FOOTNOTES

[1] *Katz v. Dole,* 709 F.2d 251, 31 FEP Cases 1521 (4th Cir. 1983); *Heelan v. Johns-Manville Corp.,* 451 F. Supp. 1382, 20 FEP Cases 251 (D. Colo. 1978); *Zabkowicz v. West Bend Co.,* 589 F. Supp 780, 35 FEP Cases 611 (E.D. Wisc. 1984); *Meyers v. I.T.T. Diversified Credit Corp.,* 527 F. Supp. 1064, 27 FEP Cases 995 (E. D. Mo. 1981).

[2] 31 FEP Cases 1521, at 1523.

[3] 641 F.2d 934, 24 FEP Cases 1155 (D.C. Cir. 1981).

[4] *Id.* at 1157.

[5] *Id.* at 1159.

[6] *Id.* at n. 8, 1159–60.

[7] 589 F. Supp. 780, 35 FEP Cases 611 (E. D. Wisc. 1984).

§4:09. —Employer's Investigation of a Complaint.

However, a full investigation of a complaint followed by prompt, appropriate remedial action is needed. Several court decisions have offered guidance on the kind of investigation that must take place.

The investigation is not complete if the investigator only asks a few questions to a few people. The classic case is *Heelan v. Johns-Manville Corp.,*[1] where an executive vice president responded to serious charges that a supervisor was repeatedly making sexual demands of a female subordinate. He telephoned the supervisor, asked him about the allegations and when they were denied, the vice president dropped the matter. The harassment continued, however, and when the plaintiff took her case to litigation, the court found "the depth and scope of these inquiries can hardly satisfy the corporation's obligation under Title VII."[2]

Likewise in *Mays v. Williamson & Sons Janitorial Services Inc.,*[3] the investigation of plaintiff's complaint was found inadequate when the president of the company "only asked his brother (the alleged harasser) to confirm or deny the charges made against him by Plaintiff and other employees, and did not conduct any investigation of (his brother's) . . . conduct."[4]

In *Delgado v. Lehman,*[5] following a complaint of sexual harassment, one meeting of the department was called to discuss the hostile working environment in the office. Suggestions made at the meeting were not followed up by any supervisor to determine whether the hostile environment had dissipated.[6] Similarly, in *Harrison v. Reed Rubber Co.,*[7] the court found that after the plaintiff's complaint, the harasser (the plant superintendent) "stayed away from her for days," but the company vice-president did not monitor the superintendent's behavior "to ascertain whether all the harassment ceased." It had not.[8] In both cases, the employer was found liable for failing to take corrective action upon notice of the sexual harassment.

The corrective action must be "reasonably calculated" to end the sexual harassment.[9] In *Barrett v. Omaha Natl. Bank,*[10] the plaintiff wanted more investigation and more corrective action than the employer took. The plaintiff went to a two-day bank conference, where a co-worker, in the presence of her supervisor, talked about sexual activity and touched her in an offensive manner."[11] The supervisor did not intervene in this situation and upon returning from the conference, plaintiff complained to a vice president.

The bank investigated the charges, determined that both the supervisor and co-worker had engaged in "inappropriate conduct" and took disciplinary measures. Within four days of the complaint, the co-worker was reprimanded for his "grossly inappropriate" conduct and placed on probation for 90 days. He was warned that any further misconduct would result in discharge. The supervisor was reprimanded for his "failure to intervene" on behalf of the plaintiff.[12] Memos detailing the disciplinary actions taken were placed in both employees' permanent personal files.[13] Nine days after her complaint, the plaintiff learned of the disciplinary actions taken.

The appellate court found that there was "ample evidence" to support the district court's conclusion here that the bank conducted a full investigation and took immediate and appropriate corrective action.[14] First, the investigation was not, as the plaintiff alleged in her lawsuit, "totally superficial,"[15] or "simply concerned" with absolving the bank.[16] The record indicated that the bank's investigator talked to the plaintiff, both of employees charged with the sexual harassment as well as other bank employees who also attended the same seminar.

Second, the appellate court also disagreed with plaintiff's allegation that the bank "took absolutely no action to ensure that her working environment would be free of future hostility."[17] The court found that the law did not require that the bank fire the two employees who it only reprimanded. The action taken was "prompt remedial action reasonably calculated to end the harassment."[18]

Some courts have indicated that with a prompt investigation and a proper corrective action, an employer has been absolved of responsibility under Title VII.[19] However, in *Henson v. City of Dundee,*[20] the court challenged the determination that an employer "may escape responsibility for sexual harassment . . . merely by taking subsequent remedial action."[21] Such corrective action may mitigate damages, "but it in no way affects an employer's liability," the court added.[22]

But other courts have questioned what triggers the need for corrective action. In *Martin v. Norbar, Inc.*,[23] the plaintiff, an over-the-road truck driver, alleged that she was sexually harassed by a co-driver on a long-distance trip. He told her "lewd stories, asked her to go to bed with him and touched her legs and thighs a number of times without her consent."[24]

When the plaintiff returned from the trip, she complained about the sexual harassment to her terminal manager and asked to be reassigned to another run in order to get away from the co-driver who was harassing her. The manager refused that request because the co-driver, when confronted with these charges, denied them all. Plaintiff quit her employment the same day.[25]

In its motion for summary judgment, the defendant employer argued that it had no duty to reassign the plaintiff who had made only one complaint of sexual harassment and it had "no way of verifying the truth of plaintiff's allegations."[26]

The defendant further argued that denying its motion for summary judgment

> . . . would be tantamount to holding that an employer must treat all allegations of sexual harassment as true, regardless of the circumstances and regardless of the fact that no supervisory or management pesonnel are involved. . . .and must take the corrective action demanded by the complaining employee regardless of the effect . . . on the employer's other employees and the employer's operation.[27]

The court responded by refusing to frame the question as whether an employer must take each complaint as true and abide by the complainant's idea of appropriate corrective action. It observed instead that "An employer may not arbitrarily choose to ignore such a serious complaint" and raised such questions as, "did the employer act appropriately in the situation, which party was the most credible—the plaintiff or the co-driver and was it reasonable for the defendant to force the plaintiff to choose between going out on the road again with (her co-driver) . . . or quitting her job."[28] Because these outstanding questions of fact were yet to be resolved, the court denied the defendant's motion for summary judgment.

Some courts have upheld prompt remedial action that results in the discharge of the harasser in sexual harassment cases when the employer's action was a result of a full investigation of the allegations. In *French v. Mead Corp.,*[29] the court held that a foreman was properly discharged when he was found to have sexually harassed at least four female subordinates. The employer's manager of labor relations had conducted a thorough investigation, including having the operations manager confront the harasser and all witnesses. See also *Crimm v. Mo. Pac R.R.,*[30] where discharge of harasser was upheld in an action by him against the employer for discrimination in violation of the Age Discrimination in Employment Act of 1967.[32]

For several courts, the determining factor has been whether the employee discharged had received a full and fair hearing prior to the discharge or upon the employee's appeal of the discharge decision. A federal bankruptcy judge in *Matter of Chapter 13,*[33] upheld the action taken to remove a bankruptcy trustee who was found at a hearing on the matter to have sexually harassed female employees. See also *Hostetter v. U.S.,*[34] where the court upheld the hearing officer's decision and its review by the federal district court because the apellate court found "substantial evidence" to support dismissal.

One court found a proper dismissal even where an employer's manager disagreed with the hearing officer's recommended penalty of a two-month suspension and fired the employee instead.[35]

However, in *Huff v. County of Butler,*[36] the court found that an employee who was discharged for sexually harassing several employees was denied due process because the disciplinary action was taken without a hearing.

Footnotes

[1] 451 F. Supp. 1382, 20 FEP Cases 251 (D. Colo. 1978).

[2] *Id.* at 1388–89.

[3] 591 F. Supp. 1518, 35 FEP Cases 1868 (E.D. Ark. 1984), *affirmed,* 775 F.2d 258, 39 FEP Cases 106 (8th Cir. 1985).

[4] 591 F. Supp. 1518, 35 FEP Cases 1868, at 1871.

[5] 43 FEP Cases 593 (E.D. Va. 1987).

[6] *Id.* at 600.

[7] 604 F. Supp. 1457, 37 FEP Cases 1545 (E.D. Mo. 1985).

[8] *Id.* at 1548.

[9] *Katz v. Dole,* 709 F.2d 251, 31 FEP Cases 1521, 1524 (4th Cir. 1983).

[10] 585 F. Supp. 635, 35 FEP Cases 209 (D.C. Wisc. 1984), *affirmed,* 726 F.2d 424, 35 FEP Cases 593 (8th Cir. 1984).

[11] 726 F. 2d 424, 35 FEP Cases 593, at 594.

[12] *Id.*

[13] *Id.* 35 FEP Cases at 588.

[14] *Id.* 35 FEP Cases at 595.

[15] *Id.* at 594.

[16] *Id.* at 595.

[17] *Id.*

[18] Citing *Katz v. Dole,* 709 F.2d 251, at 256.

[19] See *Ferguson v. duPont Co.,* 560 F. Supp. 1172, 31 FEP Cases 795 (D. Dela. 1983) and *Sapp v. City of Warner Robins,* 43 FEP Cases 486, 491 (M.D. George 1987).

[20] 682 F.2d 897, 29 FEP Cases 787 (11th Cir. 1982).

[21] *Id.* at 789, n. 19.

[22] *Id.*

[23] 537 F. Supp 1260, 30 FEP Cases 103 (S.D. Ohio 1982).

[24] *Id.* at 103.

[25] *Id.* at 103–04.

[26] *Id.* at 104.

[27] *Id.*

[28] *Id.*

[29] 33 FEP Cases 635 (S.D. Ohio 1983).

[31] 750 F. 2d 703, 36 FEP Cases 883 (8th Cir. 1984).

[32] 29 U.S.C. Section 621 (1982).

[33] 33 FEP Cases 1871, 19 BR 713 (U.S. Bnkrptcy Ct. 1982).

[34] 739 F. 2d 983, 35 FEP Cases 693 (4th Cir. 1984).

[35] *Petties v. N.Y. Dept. of Mental Retardation,* 93 App. Div.2d 960, 463 NYS2d 284, 31 FEP Cases 1164 (N.Y. App. Div. 1983).

[36] 524 F. Supp. 751, 27 FEP Cases 63 (W.D. Pa. 1981).

§4:10. Discipline or Dismissal of the Harasser.

Another question raised in these cases is how severe does the sexual harassment have to be to warrant dismissal or other serious disciplinary action. In *Jackson v. V.A.*,[1] the court found that the penalty of removal was "excessive" where there was proof of only one of five allegations of sexual harassment, no actual physical contact or *quid pro quo* and no similar past complaints about the employee.[2] The court felt instead that this employee could perform satisfactorily in a non-supervisory position and that he "could well benefit from counselling."[3]

In *Downes v. F.A.A.*,[4] the court found error in the hearing officer's decision to uphold agency action to demote and reassign manager. The sexual harassment was "trivial" and did not establish a "pattern" directed to the plaintiff or any female employee.[5] Moreover, plaintiff's evidence did not prove *quid pro quo* sexual harassment as there was no job detriment. In fact, the alleged harasser, as plaintiff's manager, repeatedly and publicly praised her professional work.[6] See *Johnson v. Perkins Restaurants, Inc.*,[7] where a 60 year old employee was properly fired for kissing a 16 year old waitress on the back of the head where the employer had an "explicit" company policy against sexual harassment which included the statement that sexual harassment was "ground for disciplinary action, including termination."[8]

In *Carosella v. U. S. Postal Service,*[9] the court upheld the discharge of a supervisor where the employer had shown by a preponderance of the evidence that he had sexually harassed six female subordinates, five of whom were probationary employees. These employees all testified that they "were concerned about keeping their jobs."[10] The court ruled it "promoted the efficiency of the federal service" to remove the supervisor for these offenses and the penalty was "both appropriate and reasonable."[11] In *Snipes v. U.S. Postal Service,*[12] the court found "substantial evidence" to support the hearing board's dismissal of a supervisor involved in four incidents of sexual harassment. Discharge was not so "harsh" or "inappropriate."[13]

An employer could also penalize its supervisors or managers, who, upon knowledge of sexual harassment, fail to make immediate corrective action. Some courts have suggested that an employer can limit its liability in a sexual harassment case if it creates such an internal sanction, but the courts have not recognized a separate legal cause of action for such inaction.[14] In *Hendrix,* the plaintiff sought to hold two supervisors *individually* liable under Title VII because they either knew or should have known that she was being sexually harassed by another supervisor and did nothing to stop it. The court concluded that "actual misfeasance, as opposed to non-feasance, is necessary for individual liability under Title VII."[15] But this case does not address imposing liability on the employer itself for a neglect of duty by its supervisors in failing to act on a complaint of sexual harassment.

While there is no clear indication that Title VII covers such inaction by an employer's supervisors, the courts have indicated that

> When the employer's supervisory personnel acquiesced and participated in such harassment, the burden on an employer seeking to avoid Title VII liability is especially heavy.[16]

And in *Bundy v. Jackson,*[17] the court stated:

> To state the all too obvious, (the supervisor who received plaintiff's complaint of sexual harassment) may have avoided all investigation precisely because he realized that proof of a practice of sexual harassment would be a serious matter for his agency indeed. Alternatively, if he in fact did consider the whole matter trivial, he was only compounding Bundy's difficulty in obtaining relief from harassment and thus, in a sense, compounding the Title VII violation.[18]

FOOTNOTES

[1] 30 FEP Cases 100 (Fed. Cir. 1985).
[2] *Id.* at 105.
[3] *Id.* at 106.
[4] 775 F.2d 288, 39 FEP Cases 70 (Fed. Cir. 1985).
[5] *Id.* at 75.
[6] *Id.* at 73.

[7] 43 FEP Cases 830 (8th Cir. 1987).

[8] *Id.* at 831.

[9] 816 F.2d 638, 43 FEP Cases 845 (Fed. Cir. 1987).

[10] *Id.* at 847.

[11] *Id.* at 849.

[12] 677 F. 2d 375, 30 FEP Cases 1257 (4th Cir. 1982).

[13] *Id.* at 1257.

[14] *Hendrix v. Fleming,* 650 F. Supp. 301, 42 FEP Cases 461 (W. D. Oklahoma, 1986).

[15] *Id.* at 462.

[16] *Katz v. Dole,* 709 F.2d 251, 31 FEP Cases 1521, cited in *Weiss v. U.S.,* 595 F. Supp. 1050, 1057 (E.D. Va. 1984).

[17] 641 F.2d 934, 24 FEP Cases 1155 (D.C. Cir. 1981).

[18] *Id.* at 1160, n. 8.

§4:11. Summary.

While the courts have not allowed a employer's policy against sexual harassment or an internal grievance procedure to be a complete defense in a sexual harassment Title VII case, those procedure and policies have been encouraged. The courts have indicated that the procedures must be fair and investigations of complaints thorough with a guarantee of immediate corrective action if warranted. Such policies and procedures, the courts have found, not only respond effectively to sexual harassment complaints, but also are an important part of the way an employer can prevent sexual harassment in the workplace.

CHAPTER FIVE

Other Legal Theories of Sexual Harassment

§5:01. Overview.

Litigators in sexual harassment cases should be aware that, while these lawsuits are most often brought under Title VII of the Civil Rights Act of 1964, the injury suffered can be redressed under both personal injury and employment discrimination law. The tort theory, in fact, is so much more recognizable, as Catharine MacKinnon points out in her book, *Sexual Harassment of Working Women,*[1] that it is surprising that sexual harassment cases first showed up under Title VII, the federal law prohibiting employment discrimination.[2]

> With a little more creativity and a little less sexism, sexual harassment might long have been a recognized tort. But it is even more interesting that without going very far out of mainstream thinking, many of the acts that comprise incidents of sexual harassment, if properly construed (this, after all, is what lawyers do), arguably fit into the traditional torts of assault and battery . . . or if sufficiently extreme, the tort of intentional infliction of emotional distress.[3]

These torts are, in fact, examples of the various causes of action that have been used to bolster the Title VII sexual harassment case ever since a Title VII remedy was first recognized in *Williams v. Saxbe.*[4] Other causes of action are under state law for breach of contract and federal constitutional rights, such as the First and Fourteenth Amendments, or statutory claims, such as Section 1983 actions.

By adding these additional state and federal claims to the Title VII cause of action, a full panoply of relief is available to the plaintiff. The tort remedy, as MacKinnon points out, focuses on the "physical and psychic damage to one's person" suffered in sexual harassment cases, a damage not compensable under Title VII. For Title VII is a statute which is more concerned with righting only the "public or shared social" wrong of having sex made part of one's employment.[5] The federal district court for the District of Columbia agreed with this distinction in *Stewart v. Thomas,*[6] when it wrote:

> The Title VII remedy for sexual harassment formulates redress in terms of equitable measures but does not offer compensation for physical and psychic damage to the person. To the extent that Title VII fails to capture the personal nature of the injury done to this plaintiff as an individual, the remedies provided by that statute fail to appreciate the relevant dimensions of the problem.[7]

The tort remedy also provides for possible punitive damages not allowed under Title VII which is compensatory in awarding its damages such as back pay, hiring, job reinstatement or promotion.[8] In addition, these tort claims may provide the plaintiff with a right to a jury trial or an alternate forum in state courts for sexual harassment cases.

The courts have allowed these additional claims to bolster a Title VII sexual harassment cause of action. For Title VII is not the exclusive remedy for injuries suffered as a result of employment discrimination. In *Johnson v. Railway Express Agency Inc.,*[9] the U.S. Supreme Court found that in Title VII, the Congress "created statutory rights against invidious discrimination" in employment and established a "comprehensive scheme for the vindication of those rights."[10] Yet despite Title VII's range and its design as a comprehensive solution to employment discrimination, the "aggrieved individual clearly is not deprived of other remedies he possesses and is not limited to Title VII in his search for relief."[11] It was clearly Congress' intent to allow an individual to pursue independently his rights under both Title VII and state and federal statutes, the Court held citing *Alexander v. Gardner-Denver Co.*[12] In particular, Congress noted in its hearings on Title VII that its remedies were "co-extensive" with rights to sue under 42 U.S.C. Section 1981.[13]

Specifically, Title VII's statutory language reads:

> Nothing in this title shall be deemed to exempt or relieve any person from any liability duty, penalty, or punishment provided by any present or future law of any State or political subdivision of a State, other than any such law which purports to require or permit the doing of any act which be an unlawful employment practice under this title.[14]

See also *Colorado Anti-Discrimination Comm'n v. Continental Airlines, Inc.*,[15] where the U.S. Supreme Court found that the federal interpretation of employment discrimination law does not control state law and states are free to provide greater protection.

In the area of Title VII sexual harassment cases, the limitation of Title VII relief has been most profoundly felt. Because of the personal nature of the injury in a case of sexual harassment, the plaintiff will find that her privacy has been invaded by the actions of others prying into the details of her personal sex life,[16] spewing obscenities and vulgar phrases at her,[17] physically touching her against her will[18] and making continual, repeated sexual advances.[19] Damages for injuries for such actions, as will be discussed in a later chapter in this book, are not compensable under Title VII, where relief is limited to back pay, reinstatement, injunctory relief or declaratory judgment.

This chapter will outline some of the additional legal claims that have been used in sexual harassment cases. While not a complete catalogue, because the range of legal causes of action are only limited by the creativity of the plaintiff attorney's imagination and ability to persuade the court, this chapter will highlight how the courts have dealt with various additional causes of action in sexual harassment cases. The chapter will also address barriers which a plaintiff must overcome and defenses that an employer may raise to these causes of action.

FOOTNOTES

[1] MacKinnon, *Sexual Harassment of Working Women,* Yale University Press (1979).

[2] 42 U.S.C. Section 2000e *et. seq.*

[3] MacKinnon, at 159.

[4] 413 F. Supp. 654 (D.D.C. 1976).

[5] MacKinnon, at 88.

[6] 30 FEP Cases 1609 (D.D.C. 1982).

[7] *Id.* at 1613.

[8] MacKinnon, at 88.

[9] 421 U.S. 454 (1975).

[10] *Id.* at 457–58.

[11] *Id.* at 459.

[12] 415 U.S. 36, 48 (1974).

[13] 421 U.S. 454, at 459.

[14] 42 U.S.C. Section 2000e–7.

[15] 372 U.S. 714, 1 FEP Cases 25 (1963).

[16] *Ambrose v. U.S. Steel Corp.,* 39 FEP Cases 30 (D. Col. 1985).

[17] *Rabidue v. Osceola Refining Co.,* 584 F. Supp. 419, 36 FEP Cases 183 (E.D. Mich. 1984), *affirmed,* 805 F.2d 611, 42 FEP Cases 631 (6th Cir. 1986); *Zabkowicz v. West Bend Co.,* 589 F. Supp. 780, 35 FEP Cases 611 (E.D. Wic. 1984).

[18] *Robson v. Eva's Supermarket,* 538 F. Supp 857, 30 FEP Cases 1212 (N.D. Ohio 1982)

[19] *Heelan v. Johns-Mansville Corp.,* 451 F. Supp. 1382, 20 FEP Cases 251 (D. Col. 1978).

§5:02. Pendent Jurisdiction.

The first barrier to bringing causes of action under state law into a Title VII sexual harassment lawsuit is the discretion of the district court to exercise pendent jurisdiction over state claims. First articulated by the U.S. Supreme Court in *United Mine Workers v. Gibbs,*[1] the Court set forth a two-prong test for determining the exercise of pendent jurisdiction. The first prong is whether the court has the power over the state law claims and second is whether the court in its discretion should entertain them.[2]

A court has the power to hear the claims if 1) there is a federal claim with "substance sufficient to confer subject matter jurisdiction on the court; 2) the state and federal claims "derive from a common nucleus of operative fact"; and 3) "the plaintiff's claims are such that he would ordinarily be expected to try them all in one judicial proceeding."[3]

If the court has the power to hear the claims, then the court can use a number of factors to guide its exercise of discretion; the principle of which are judicial economy, convenience and fairness to litigants. If these are not present, "a federal court should hesitate to exercise jurisdiction over state claims."[4]

Furthermore, if the "state issues substantially predominate, whether in terms of proof, of the scope of the issues raised, or of the comprehensiveness of the remedy sought," the state claims should be left to the state courts for resolution.[5]

The Supreme Court has held that

> . . . it is evident from *Gibbs* that pendent state law claims are not always, or even almost always, to be dismissed and not adjudicated. On the contrary, given advantages of economy and convenience and no unfairness to litigants, *Gibbs* contemplates adjudication of those claims.[6]

In sexual harassment Title VII cases, several courts have properly exercised pendent jurisdiction over state law claims. In *Phillips v. Smalley Maint. Services,*[7] the appellate court upheld the district court exercising pendent jurisdiction over the state law claims. The appellate court found that "[c]learly the district court had the *power* to hear the state law issues. The federal Title VII claim was one of substance, evidenced in large part by the fact that plaintiff prevailed . . . and all claims arose out of the same set of operative facts."[8] Furthermore, the appellate court noted that to refuse to exercise pendent jurisdiction in this case would have required "substantially duplicative proceedings in federal and state courts. Witnesses would have been forced to testify twice to the same facts."[9] In *Guyette v. Stauffer Chemical Co.,*[10] the court exercised pendent jurisdiction over the state law claims indicating that

> A sexual harassment theory of recovery under Title VII bears distinct similarities to, and to a large extent arises out of, common law torts such as assault and battery and intentional interference with contractual relations . . . . . Consequently, the evidence necessary to prove a Title VII harassment violation overlaps that necessary to prove underlying state law torts to a significant degree.[11]

The court concluded:

> To require the state claims to be tried in a separate forum would be duplicative and wasteful of the time and resources of the courts and litigants alike.[12]

However, several federal courts have dismissed state law pendent claims when the state in which the claim is made does not recognize the cause of action alleged. For example, in *Collins v. Pfizer, Inc.,*[13] the court dismissed plaintiff's claim for negligent infliction of emotional distress where Connecticut law recognizes only *intentional* infliction of emotional distress. See also discussions in *Phillips v. Smalley Maint. Services,*[14] where the court did not dismiss a state law claim because Alabama law does recognize a cause of action for tortious invasion of the right of privacy, and, *Robson v. Eva's Supermarket,*[15] where a state law claim was upheld because Ohio law does recognize causes of action for both intentional and negligent infliction of emotional distress.

Footnotes

[1] 383 U.S. 715, 725, 86 S.Ct. 1130, 1138, 16 L.Ed.2d 218 (1966).

[2] See also *Moor v. County of Alameda*, 411 U.S. 693 (1973).

[3] 383 U.S. 715, 86 S. Ct. 1130, 16 L. Ed.2d 218, at 726.

[4] *Id.* at 726.

[5] *Id.* at 727.

[6] *Hagas v. Lavine,* 415 U.S. 528 (1974).

[7] 711 F.2d 1524, 32 FEP Case 977, 980–81 (8th Cir. 1983).

[8] *Id.*
[9] *Id.*
[10] 518 F. Supp. 521, 26 FEP Cases 32 (S.D. Geo. 1985).
[11] Id. at 636.
[12] Id. at 636.
See also *Wimberly v. Shoney's Inc.*, 38 FEP Cases 932 (S.D. Geo. 1985), citing *Phillips* at 933.
[13] 39 FEP Cases 1316, 1331–32 (D. Conn. 1985).
[14] 711 F.2d 1524, 32 FEP Cases 975, 981 (11th Cir. 1983).
[15] 538 F. Supp. 857, 30 FEP Cases 1212, 1217 (N.D. Ohio 1982).

§5:03. Tort Claims.

Given the similarities between Title VII claims and tort actions mentioned above, it is not uncommon to find tort law claims alleged along with a Title VII cause of action. See Title VII cases including *Phillips v. Smalley Maint. Services,*[1] where battery and tortious invasion of the right of privacy were alleged; *Robson v. Eva's Supermarket,*[2] where negligent and intentional infliction of emotional distress were alleged; *Collins v. Pfizer, Inc.,*[3] where negligent infliction of emotional distress was alleged; *Wimberly v. Shoney's Inc.,*[4] where plaintiff alleged assault and battery and intentional infliction of emotional distress; *Howard University v. Best,*[5] where plaintiff alleged intentional infliction of emotional distress and defamation; *Guyette v. Stauffer Chemical Co.,*[6] where assault and battery, intentional and negligent infliction of emotional distress, negligence, gross negligence and intentional interference with contract rights were alleged; *Shaffer v. National Can Corp.,*[7] where plaintiff alleged intentional infliction of emotional distress; *Cummings v. Walsh Construction Co.,*[8] where intentional infliction of emotional distress, tort of outrage, interference with contract right and invasion of privacy were alleged; *Epps v. Riley,*[9] where plaintiff alleged intentional infliction of emotional distress; *Stewart v. Thomas,*[10] where plaintiff alleged tort of outrage and intentional infliction of emotional distress; *Ukarish v. Magnesium Elektron,*[11] where plaintiff alleged conspiracy for intentional infliction of emotional distress, interference with contractual relationship and negligent supervision.

In examining these tort claims, the courts have looked to see if the plaintiff has alleged a *prima facie* case against an individual supervisor or employee. The most extensive discussion of these two aspects of the tort claims appears in the court's decision on defendant's motion for summary judgment in *Rogers v. Loews L'Enfant Plaza Hotel.*[12] Oddly, *Rogers* is a tort action, not a Title VII case, that stayed in federal court after the Title VII claim was moot and the court held that a "case in controversy" for federal court jurisdiction still existed.[13]

FOOTNOTES

[1] 711 F.2d 1524, 32 FEP Cases 977 (11th Cir. 1983).
[2] 538 F. Supp. 857, 30 FEP Cases 1212 (N.D. Ohio, 1982).
[3] 39 FEP Cases 1316 (D. Conn. 1985).
[4] 38 FEP Cases 933 (S.D. Geo. 1985).
[5] 482 A2d 958, 36 FEP Cases 482 (D.C. Cir. 1984).
[6] 518 F. Supp. 521, 26 FEP Cases 634 (D. N.J. 1981).
[7] 565 F. Supp. 909, 34 FEP Cases 172 (E. D. Pa. 1983).
[8] 561 F. Supp. 872, 31 FEP Cases 930 (S.D. Geo. 1983).
[9] 30 FEP Cases 1632 (D.D.C. 1982).
[10] 538 F. Supp. 89, 30 FEP Cases 1609 (D.D.C. 1982).
[11] 31 FEP Cases 1315 (D. N.J. 1983).
[12] 526 F.Supp. 523, 29 FEP Cases 828 (D.D.C. 1981).
[13] *Id.* at 833–34.

See also *Ford v. Revlon,* 43 FEP Cases 213 (Ariz. Supreme Court 1987), a tort action tried in Arizona state court.).

§5:04. Right to Privacy.

In *Rogers v. Loews L'Enfant Plaza Hotel,*[1] the court recognizes a right to privacy—the right "to be let alone," citing W. Prosser, The Law of Torts, Section 117 at 804 (4th ed. 1971).[2] In support of this claim, the plaintiff alleged acts by defendant supervisor where he would call her at home or on duty while at work and make "sarcastic, leering comments about her personal and sexual life."[3] The court found that although in most circumstances it is obviously not an intrusion to call someone at home or at a place of business, in this particular situation with allegations of sexual harassment in plaintiff's personal and professional life, the pleadings are "sufficient to indicate an intrusion into a sphere from which plaintiff . . . could reasonably expect that defendant (supervisor) . . . should be excluded."[4] The court denied defendant's motion to dismiss this claim.

In *Cummings v. Walsh Construction Co.*,[5] the court granted defendant's motion for summary judgment on the tort claim of "invasion of privacy" because the plaintiff had missed proving an essential element, a "physical intrusion, analogous to a trespass, into a plaintiff's private affairs, seclusion or solitude."[6]

Plaintiff contended the intrusion was that her supervisor engaged in sexual intercourse with her, but the defendant claimed that this was not the kind of "physical intrusion" contemplated. The court responded by finding another more fatal defect in plaintiff's allegations, that she had not shown that acts of sexual intercourse were "unwanted, uninvited and unwarranted."[7] The court indicated, "there does not seem to be any issue that plaintiff did not desire to have relations with (her supervisor) . . . but it is also altogether apparent that she willingly had sex with him." The court notes that when the plaintiff listed her sexual encounters with her supervisor on the job, she did not indicate that she was forced by any "threats" or "duress" to submit to sexual intercourse with him. The court concluded: ". . . [P]laintiff had the alternative of outright refusal. She did not choose that path, and in so doing, waived whatever right to privacy she had as to her personal seclusion or privacy."[8]

In both cases, the plaintiff properly brought the tort claim against the individual supervisor.

Footnotes

[1] 526 F. Supp. 523, 29 FEP Cases 828, at 830. (D.D.C. 1981).

[2] *Id.* at n.6.

[3] *Id.* at 828.

[4] *Id.* at 831.

[5] 561 F. Supp. 872, 31 FEP Cases 930 (S.D. Ga. 1983).

[6] *Id.* at 937.
[7] *Id.*
[8] *Id.* at 938.

§5:05. Assault and Battery.

In *Rogers v. Loews L'Enfant Plaza Hotel,*[1] the court found that the plaintiff had stated "adequate claims" to defeat a motion to dismiss an assault and battery cause of action. Those claims included that her supervisor had touched her or pulled at her hair because she refused his sexual advances.

Examining these claims in the assault cause of action, the court found that a plaintiff must show "apprehension of a harmful or offensive contact with a person." That apprehension must be one which would "normally be aroused in the mind of a reasonable person and apparent ability and opportunity to carry out the threat immediately must be present." The plaintiff properly showed that she was "frightened and embarrassed" by her supervisor's actions and was in "immediate apprehension of an offensive contact."[2]

As to the battery claim, which had an additional element of an "offensive contact without consent, the court also found "sufficient" allegations to survive a motion to dismiss.[3]

This action was properly brought against the supervisor.

Footnotes

[1] 526 F. Supp. 523, 29 FEP Cases 828, at 831. (D.D.C. 1981).
[2] Id. at 831.
[3] Id. at 832.

§5:06. Intentional Infliction of Emotional Distress.

In *Rogers v. Loews L'Enfant Plaza Hotel,*[1] the court found a cause of action for intentional emotional distress. For a *prima facie* case to be established, the plaintiff must show "wanton, outrageous in the extreme or especially calculated to cause serious mental distress."[2] The conduct must have been intentional so that "any reasonable person would have known that emotional distress would result."[3]

Here the plaintiff alleged that she was "frightened and embarrassed" because of her supervisor's sexual suggestions and advances which she found "distressful and unwanted." After she rejected these advances, her supervisor excluded her from meetings, used abusive language and belittled her in public. He advised her that he would do everything in his power to have her fired. Even though she complained to his superiors about his conduct, at no time was the matter resolved to her satisfaction.[4]

The court ruled that in her complaint, the plaintiff has "clearly alleged conditions and circumstances which are beyond mere insults, indignities and petty oppressions and which if proved, could be construed as outrageous."[5] The court found that emotional distress and physical harm could "reasonably" result from the supervisor's conduct as well as from the conduct of the employer in not responding to the plaintiff's plight.[6]

The court in *Ford v. Revlon,*[7] echoed the ruling in *Rogers* when it found liability for intentional infliction of emotional distress in the employer's "outrageous" conduct of not timely resolving plaintiff's complaints of serious sexual harassment by her supervisor. This harassment included physical assaults and vulgar remarks in the presence of other employees which the plaintiff brought to the employer's attention in May, 1980. In October, 1981, Revlon finally terminated the supervisor, but not before he made physical threats "that he wanted to destroy her" and the plaintiff had attempted suicide.[8] The court found "ample" evidence, both medical and otherwise, that the sexual harassment in her "stressful work environment" caused plaintiff's emotional distress and her physical complications.[9]

In addition, the court found the employer liable even though the jury did not find the individual supervisor whose actions constituted the sexual harassment liable for intentional infliction of emotional distress. The court wrote: "We believe that Revlon's failure to investigate Ford's complaint was independent of (the supervisor's) . . . abusive treatment of Ford." The court cited

Davis v. U.S. Steel Corp.,[10] a case factually similar in which a corporation was held liable for intentional infliction of emotional distress for failing to act on a sexual harassment complaint.

FOOTNOTES

[1] 526 F. Supp. 523, 29 FEP Cases 828, at 832 (D.D.C. 1981).
[2] Id. at 832.
[3] *Id.*
[4] *Id.* at 833.
[5] *Id.*
[6] *Id.*
[7] 734 P.2d 580, 43 FEP Cases 213 (Ariz. Sup. Ct. 1987).
[8] *Id.* at 214–215.
[9] *Id.* at 217.
[10] 779 F.2d 209, 211, 39 FEP Cases 955 (4th Cir. 1985).

§5:07. Tort of Outrage.

This tort claim is the same as the tort of intentional infliction of emotional distress.[1]

FOOTNOTES

[1] *Stewart v. Thomas*, 538 F. Supp. 89, 30 FEP Cases 1609 (D.D.C. 1982).
See also *Cummings v. Walsh Construction Co.*, 561 F. Supp. 872, 31 FEP Cases 930 (S.D. Geo. 1983) where court held that tort of outrage is not recognized in Georgia.

§5:08. Negligent Infliction of Emotional Distress.

As to the tort of negligent infliction of emotional distress, although not alleged in *Rogers*, the court found that this tort, unlike its intentional counterpart, requires a physical injury.[1] In *Collins v. Pfizer, Inc.*,[2] the plaintiff's tort claim for negligent infliction of emotional distress was dismissed for a number of reasons, including that there was no competent medical testimony of any physical injury as a result of the sexual harassment, except maybe a back injury the plaintiff had sustained some years before trial.

In *Robson v. Eva's Supermarket,*[3] the plaintiff's claim for negligent infliction of emotional distress was that an employee had grabbed her arm and bruised it. The court denied defendant's motion for summary judgment and found that whether the bruise rises to the level of that physical injury necessary for negligent behavior "may be academic." There were facts alleged that might be "wanton or outrageous" and "damages for emotional pain, fright and humiliation could be awarded by the trier of fact."[4]

FOOTNOTES

[1] 526 F. Supp. 523, 29 FEP Cases 828, at 832 (D.D.C. 1981).
[2] 39 FEP Cases 1316 (D. Conn. 1985).
[3] 538 F. Supp. 857, 30 FEP Cases 1212 (N.D. Ohio 1982).
[4] *Id.* at 1217–18.

§5:09. Interference with Contract.

The plaintiff in *Cummings v. Walsh Construction Co.,*[1] characterized this tort action as "conduct of defendant's supervisory personnel (that) interfered with her contractual employment rights, among them, the right to work without fear of sexual harassment."[2] However, the court found that the claim was not brought against the proper party—the supervisor and explained: "A claim for tortious interference should be brought against the individuals who interfered, not against the employer." The court granted summary judgment to the defendant on this claim.[3]

FOOTNOTES

[1] 561 F. Supp 872, 31 FEP Cases 930 (S.D. Geo. 1983).
[2] *Id.* at 937.
[3] *Id.*

See also *Guyette v. Stauffer Chemical Co.,* 26 FEP Cases 634, 638 (D. N.J. 1981), where court found that at least with respect to the individual defendants, plaintiff had stated a legally cognizable cause of action, citing *Kriazi v. Western Electric Co.* 461 F. Supp 894, 950, 18 FEP Cases 924 (D. N.J. 1978).

§5:10. Wrongful Discharge.

In an early reported sexual harassment case, the court in *Monge v. Beebe Rubber Co.,*[1] held that when an employee is terminated for refusing the sexual demands of her supervisor, she has a cause of action for breach of an oral contract of employment. The court, in this case of a plaintiff who was harassed by her foreman because she refused to go out with him and was then eventually fired, carved an exception to the employment at-will doctrine.

Tradtionally, an employer could discharge any employee at any time for any reason or for no reason at all, absent a contractual agreement. In *Monge,* the court balanced the employer's interest "in running his business as he sees fit" against the interest of the employee in retaining his job and the public's interest "in maintaining a proper balance between the two."[2] The court held that when an employer is motivated to terminate a contract of employment at will "by bad faith or malice or based on retaliation," this is not "in the best interest of the economic system or the public good and constitutes a breach of employment contract."[3]

On appeal to the New Hampshire Supreme court however, was the issue of whether there was sufficient evidence to support a jury's finding in the trial court that the defendant, through its agents, acted maliciously in terminating the plaintiff. The Supreme Court found that the jury could draw a "not-so-subtle inference" from the evidence before it that this was so.

> The foreman's overtures and the capricious firing at 2 a.m., the seeming manipulation of job assignments, and the apparent connivance of the personnel manager in this course of events all support the jury's conclusion that the dismissal was maliciously motivated.[4]

In *Monge,* it was to the plaintiff's advantage to be in a state court, where a state could clearly decide as a matter of public policy to abrogate the employment at-will doctrine. The plaintiff in *Wolk v. Saks Fifth Avenue,*[5] was not similarly advantaged. In a federal court on diversity jurisdiction (out-of-state defendant), the plaintiff urged the court to follow the "clear trend" and find that an employer has to discharge an employee "in good faith" and only "with good cause."[6] The federal court, however, found no indication that Pennsylvania courts intended to follow that trend and wrote: "Absent such a declaration on the part of the state courts, a federal tribunal sitting in diversity is not empowered to take this step for the state courts."[7]

The federal court in *Zywicki v. Moxness Products,*[8] was not so reluctant to shape such an exception for the state of Wisconsin. The federal court noted that, while the Wisconsin Supreme Court had not spoken on the issue, the state appellate court had embraced the concept of a "public policy exception" to the at-will employment doctrine.[9]

However, the court in *Zywicki* found other reasons to dismiss plaintiff's claims for wrongful discharge. First, the court was convinced that Wisconsin, like several other states, would not allow the common-law wrongful discharge actions if statutory remedies already had been provided a remedy for the violations involved.[10] Second, the court was not convinced that the allegations in plaintiff's complaint rose to a level to sustain a wrongful discharge claim in Wisconsin. The court concluded: "An employer's mere unreasonable, unfair, and inconsistent conduct is not actionable."[11]

A decision similar to the ruling in *Zywicki* under Wisconsin law was made by the Third Circuit Court of Appeals in *Wolk v. Saks Fifth Avenue.*[12] That decision was that the Pennsylvania Human Rights Act, which provided remedies for employment discrimination, supplanted the common-law claim for wrongful discharge in a sexual harassment case. See also *Shaffer v. National Can Corp.,*[13] also finding that Pennsylvania Human Relations Act has the exclusivity of its remedies and *Lui v. Intercontinental Hotels Corp. (Hawaii),*[14] where plaintiff's constructive discharge claim is barred by Hawaii's employment discrimination statute.

On the other hand, in *Holien v. Sears, Roebuck & Co.,*[15] the court found that the Oregon legislature in enacting its Fair Employment Practices Act had no intent to eliminate the common-law remedy of wrongful discharge. The court found "no inherent inconsistency between the availability of equitable relief through a statutory suit and legal remedies through a common-law action for wrongful discharge."[16]

Other courts have drawn other distinctions in dismissing state claims of wrongful discharge. In Illinois, the implied covenants of good faith and fair dealing in employment contracts do not extend to at-will employees. See *Scott v. Sears Roebuck & Co.*,[17] where plaintiff admitted that she never signed a written contract other than an employment application.

FOOTNOTES

[1] 114 N.H. 130, 16 A.2d 549 (N.H. Sup. Ct. 1974).
[2] *Id.* at 551.
[3] *Id.*
[4] *Id.* at 552.
[5] 728 F.2d 221, 34 FEP Cases 193 (3rd Cir. 1984).
[6] *Id.* at 195.
[7] *Id.*
[8] 31 FEP Cases 1348 (E.D. Wisc. 1983).
[9] *Id.* at 1349.
[10] *Id.* at 1349, citations to other cases omitted.
[11] *Id.*
[12] 728 F.2d 221, 34 FEP Cases 193 (3rd Cir. 1984).
[13] 565 F. Supp. 909, 34 FEP Cases 172 (E.D. Pa. 1983).
[14] 634 F. Supp. 684, 688 (D. Hawaii 1986).
[15] 298 Ore. 76, 689 P2d 1292, 36 FEP Cases 137 (Or. Sup. Ct. 1984).
[16] *Id.* at 145–46.
[17] 798 F.2d 210, 41 FEP Cases 805, 809 (7th Cir. 1986).

§5:11. Defense of the Worker's Compensation Bar.

Some state courts have found that state worker's compensation statutes serve as a bar to pendent state law claims for assault and battery and other intentional torts. This is premised on the idea that worker's compensation laws are the exclusive remedy in a state for work-related injuries.

In *Harrison v. Reed Rubber Co.*,[1] the district court dismissed the plaintiff's three state tort claims on a motion for summary judgment by the defendant in a sexual harassment complaint. She alleged that she was subjected to sexual harassment by a male employee, despite her efforts to terminate his attention and despite her requests to her employer to take appropriate corrective action. As a result, the plaintiff alleges she was eventually demoted to another position.

The plaintiff's claims for assault and battery, and negligent and intentional infliction of emotional distress were found to be barred by the Missouri worker's compensation law, "which does not supplement the common law but is wholly substitutional in character and creates entirely new rights and remedies."[2] Here, the court held that the injuries complained of occurred at the plaintiff's place of employment and arose out of and in the scope of plaintiff's employment.[3]

In *Cummings v. Walsh Construction Co.*,[4] the claim of plaintiff, a female laborer on a construction site, for intentional infliction of emotional distress was not barred by the Georgia worker's compensation statute. The court reached this decision because it found that the "mental distress" alleged by the plaintiff can be classified under the Georgia worker's compensation law as neither an "injury" or an "occupational disease."[5] Georgia's law does not find "mental trauma alone brought about solely by psychic stimulus" compensable. The court also found it was not an occupational disease because the mental distress alleged here is "of a type to which the general public is exposed." The court observed: "Egregious, reprehensible conduct causing emotional trauma occurs both on and off job sites to workers and non-workers alike. There is nothing so peculiar about the construction trade and its working conditions that makes emotional distress a risk not found in everyday life."[6]

An assault and battery claim against an employer and its agents was not found to be barred by the Missouri Worker's Compensation Law, at least for purpose of a dismissal motion at the early stages of the case.[7] There, the court found that since the worker's compensation law "affords no remedy in this case, it obviously cannot operate to exclude other possible remedies."[8] This is true because the question here is did the assault arise out of plaintiff's employment? If yes, then the acts are compensable under worker's compensation. If not, then the injuries and the damages sustained can be the basis for a state tort claim for assault and battery. The court ruled that questions of fact still exist as to whether the assault was the result of "purely personal and private quarrels," or arose out of the plaintiff's employment.[9] Secondly, the injuries claimed, emotional distress, nervousness and damage to her reputation, may not be injuries encompassed by the state worker's compensation law.[10]

Finally, the court stated: "This court is simply not prepared to say that a female who goes to work in what is apparently a predominantly male workplace should reasonably expect sexual harassment as part of her job, so as to bring any such injuries under the Worker's Compensation Law."[11]

In *Bennet v. Furr's Cafeteria,*[12] the court allied itself with the decision in *Pryor.* There, the plaintiff alleged repeated acts of sexual assault and harassment in a state tort claim for assault and battery. The acts occurred when the plaintiff and her supervisor were in a motel and on the road during inspection trips. The court denied the defendant's motion for summary judgment finding a question of fact as to the job-relatedness of the injuries. That is, did plaintiff's injuries arise out of and in the course of her employment with Furr's.[13]

But the court in *Lui v. Intercontinental Hotels Corp.* (*Hawaii*),[14] took issue with the result in *Pryor.* The *Lui* court saw the Hawaii workers' compensation law adopting a more liberal approach to the nature of the term "injury."[15] Under this approach, "injury falls under workers' compensation if it 'reasonably appears to have flowed from conditions under which the employee is required to work.' "[16] In fact, only a "tenuous" connection to work is required: "The only consideration should have been whether the attack in fact was aggravated or accelerated by the work activity."[17] The court concluded that the Hawaii worker's compensation law was plaintiff's exclusive remedy for her injuries which she alleged were "multiple sexual assault and batteries upon Plaintiff and other sexual harassment during working hours."[18]

The results in *Cummings, Pryor* and *Bennett* as opposed to the decision in *Lui,* show how the ability of employees to recover has greatly increased under worker's compensation laws across the country. *Cummings, Pryor* and *Bennett,* all decided in the early 1980's, reflect in their decisions earlier perceptions that only job-related physical injuries were compensable. *Lui* reflects later expansion of the laws to compensate non-physical injuries, especially stress-related injuries.

The cases also reflect the current dilemma of the worker who has been a victim of sexual harassment. This worker, in some ways, would rather have a jury hear her claims for pain and suffering, humiliation and embarassment because she may receive a higher monetary award than she could receive under the worker's compensation law in her state. On the other hand, a worker who prefers to file her sexual harassment claim in the worker's compensation system, would want the law to recognize and compensate stress-related non-physical injuries, the kind of injury she would most likely suffer in a sexual harassment case.

The dilemma of an employee subjected to sexual harassment was resolved in one way by a federal district court in Alaska in a sexual harassment case.[19] The court held there that plaintiff's recovery under worker's compensation does not bar a claim under Title VII.

Footnotes

1 603 F. Supp. 1456, 137 FEP Cases 1545 (E.D. Mo. 1984).
2 *Id.* at 1545.
3 *Id.*
4 561 F. Supp. 8732, 31 FEP Cases 930 (S.D. Georgia 1983).
5 *Id.* at 935.
6 *Id.* at 935.
7 585 F. Supp. 311 (W.D. Mo. 1984).
8 *Id.* at 314.
9 *Id.* at 315.
10 *Id.* at 316.
11 *Id.*
12 549 F. Supp. 887, 30 FEP Cases 93 (D. Colorado 1982).
13 *Id.* at 95.

[14] 634 F. Supp. 684 (D. Hawaii 1986).
[15] *Id.* at 687.
[16] *Id.* citations omitted.
[17] *Id.* at 687–688 citations omitted.
[18] *Id.* at 685.
[19] *Jeppsen v. Wunnicke,* 611 F. Supp. 78, 37 FEP Cases 994 (D. Alaska 1985).

§5:12. Federal Claims.

Beside state law tort and contract causes of action, several plaintiffs have alleged claims under the U.S. Constitution and federal statutes.

The constitutional claims have been utilized in several reported cases of sexual harassment under Title VII. In *Otto v. Heckler,*[1] the plaintiff alleged constitutional violations and common-law torts by a supervisor who sexually harassed her. On the constitutional claims, she alleged a violation of her fourteenth amendment right to privacy and her fifth amendment right to equal protection of the law. The trial court dismissed all but her Title VII claim, which was later settled.

In so dismissing her federal and state claims, the trial court relied on the authority of *Brown v. GSA,*[2] which held that Title VII "provides the exclusive judicial remedy for claims of discrimination in federal employment."[3]

But the appellate court reiterated its statement in *White v. GSA,*[4] that Title VII does not preclude separate remedies for "unconstitutional action other than discrimination" and found that the plaintiff had alleged that her constitutional claims resulted, not from discriminatory employment practices remediable under Title VII, "but from non-job and non-personnel actions."[5]

Yet, the plaintiff's case was flawed. The appellate court found no constitution violation under *Bivens v. Six Unknown Named Agents,*[6] where a federal agent must act within the "parameters" of his or her authority when causing the injury. Furthermore, the claim that her supervisor violated her right to privacy "by making defamatory remarks about her sexuality, by following her, by telephoning her and placing her in fear of sexual abuse,"[7] was not an invasion of a constitutional right but "rather sounded in tort."[8]

> Her supervisor's conduct does not amount to a governmental intrusion into the intimacies of married life. *Griswold v. Connecticut*, 381 U.S. 479, 485–86 (1965).[9]

Two other constitutional claims—violation of constitutionally protected liberty interest in her reputation[10] and her fifth amendment right to equal protection—were dismissed because the court found they were identical to her Title VII claim and she had already received relief under that claim.[11]

In *Woerner v. Brzeczek,*[12] the plaintiffs' constitutional claims did survive defendant's motion to dismiss. The plaintiffs, two police officers, alleged two Fourteenth Amendment claims under 42 U.S.C. Section 1983: that the one female plaintiff (Woerner) was sexually harassed by her supervisor in violation of the equal protection clause and both plaintiffs were retaliated against in violation of their First Amendment rights incorporated into the Fourteenth Amendment.

The court analyzed the equal protection claim, finding first, that the sexual harassment was sex discrimination under the constitution because "sex discrimination exists whenever a demand is made on one employee that would not be made of an employee of the opposite sex."[13] The court concluded here that the treatment Woerner received (such as her supervisor's sexual advances), would not have been directed toward male police officers.[14] Second, the court noted that Woerner alleged proper state action as the police officers and administrators all acted "under color" of state law. Finally, under constitutional scrutiny, citing *Craig v. Boren,*[15] the court held that Woerner had charged acts "entirely unrelated to a legitimate governmental objective" and the court added: "No such legitimate objective is served when a supervisor propositions a patrol officer sexually."[16]

As to the First Amendment claim, the court found a cause of action in plaintiffs' allegations that because of their complaints about the sexual harassment of Woerner, they had been penalized and harassed by the supervisor, a deputy chief and a medical services coordinator. In addition, the police superintendent took no action on any of their complaints.[17]

As to other federal statutory claims, several courts have found that actions for sexual harassment under 42 U.S.C. Section 1981 were barred because that section covers race not sex discrimination. Some plaintiffs have also alleged "conspiracy" charges under 42 U.S.C. Section 1985(3), a federal statute. The most successful case was *Kyriazi v. Western Electric,*[18] in which the court found that the plaintiff had established the existence of a conspiracy among the employer and five named individual employees "to deprive her of her federally-protected right to be secure of employment discrimination on the basis of sex."[19] She proved that her coworkers jointly agreed to ridicule and harass her as a woman, that her supervisors tacitly encouraged this conduct "by deliberately choosing to overlook it" and that Western, "through its agents, was a party to and carried out the objects of the conspiracy, which was ultimately the termination of Kyriazi."[20]

FOOTNOTES

[1] 39 FEP Cases 1754 (9th Cir. 1986).

[2] 425 U.S. 820, 835, 12 FEP Cases 1361 (1976).

[3] Otto v. Heckler, 39 FEP Cases 1754, 1755 (9th Cir. 1986.)

[4] 652 F.2d 913, 917, 26 FEP Cases 974 (9th Cir. 1981).

[5] 39 FEP Cases 1754, at 1756.

[6] 403 U.S. 388 (1971).

[7] 39 FEP Cases 1754, at 1756.

[8] *Id.*

[9] *Id.*

[10] Citing *Paul v. Davis,* 424 U.S. 693, 701–710 (1976).

[11] *Id.*

[12] 519 F. Supp 517, 26 FEP Cases 897 (N.D. Ill. 1981).

[13] *Id.* at 898.

[14] *Id.*

[15] 429 U.S. 190, 197 (1976).

[16] *Id.*

[17] *Id.* at 898–99.

For additional cases on constitutional claims, see also *Estate of Scott v.*

deLeon, 37 FEP Cases 563 (E.D. Mich. 1985); *Skadegaard v. Farell,* 33 FEP Cases 1528, 1536–37 (D. N.J. 1984).

[18] 461 F. Supp. 894, 18 FEP Cases 924 (D. N.J. 1978).

[19] *Id.* at 964.

[20] *Id.*

§5:13. State Statutory Claims.

State laws that prohibit employment discrimination also prohibit sexual harassment. Some states have specific provisions that prohibit sexual harassment.[1]

State human rights laws are usually interpreted by relying on federal court decisions interpreting provisions of Title VII that are similar to state law provisions.[2] Therefore, states have followed Title VII jurisprudence in finding that sexual harassment is sex discrimination.[3]

FOOTNOTES

[1] See Connecticut C.G.S. Section 46a–60(a)(8).

[2] See *Michigan Department of Civil Rights v. General Motors,* 93 Mich. App. 366, 375, 26 FEP Cases 326 (1979).

[3] *Rabidue v. Osceola Refining Co.,* 584 F. Supp. 419, 36 FEP Cases 183 (E.D. Mich. 1984), *affirmed,* 805 F.2d 611, 42 FEP Cases 631 (6th Cir. 1986); *Sand v. Johnson,* 33 FEP Cases 716 (E.D. Mich. 1982); *Continental Can Co.,* 22 FEP Cases 1808 (Minn. Supreme Court 1980).

§5:14. Unemployment Compensation Benefits.

Beside litigation in state and federal court, state administrative remedies exist for employees who have been sexually harassed and seek unemployment compensation benefits. Under the statutory and regulatory schemes in several states, employees who have been subjected to sexual harassment in employment have been afforded unemployment compensation benefits.

Many states confer upon employees a right to unemployment compensation unless the employee leaves voluntarily without sufficient cause connected with the job.[1] If the employer asserts that the claimant is ineligible because he or she quit work without good cause, the burden of proof rests on the claimant to establish eligibility.[2]

A few state courts have ruled directly that sexual harassment is "good cause" for leaving suitable work voluntarily.[3]

In *Franklin v. Administrator,*[4] the court granted unemployment benefits to a claimant who voluntarily quit her job after an employer lifted her skirt and patted her buttocks.

An unemployment compensation adjudicator must subjectively determine "good cause" by applying a "reasonable person" test. *Farfado v. Morgan.*[5] " 'Good cause' includes those situations that would motivate the average able-bodied and qualified worker to give up his or her employment with certain wage rewards in order to enter the ranks of the unemployed."[6] Under this standard, the claimant must show that the conditions under which she was expected to work were unreasonable. Notwithstanding this requirement, a woman is not expected to sacrifice her personal integrity to remain at a job. The law cannot demand that an employee "sacrifice all other economic objectives, ethnic or sexual slurs, or personal abuse, for fear that abandoning an oppressive situation will disqualify the worker from unemployment benefits."[7]

Moreover, it is well established that discrimination against an employee in violation of state or federal employment law constitutes "good cause" for quitting one's job.[8] More specifically, illegal discrimination on the basis of race or sex constitutes "good cause" as well.[9]

Finally, "good cause" exists whenever an employer singles out a particular employee and abuses or harasses her for any reason.[10] If the work conditions become intolerable as a result of that harassment, an employee has good cause of leaving and is entitled to unemployment compensation benefits.[11] Resignation is a reasonable manner of responding to personal abuse.[12]

Thus, whether the sexual harassment is viewed as illegal sex discrimination or as harassment, it should be considered "good cause" to voluntarily quit one's job under the "reasonable person" standard.

As noted above, the "reasonable person's" standard for deciding "good cause" for voluntarily leaving one's employment is measured by a subjective criteria. In *Caldwell v. Hodgeman,*[13] a decision by a Massachusetts district court, the court elaborated on this criteria. The female claimant alleged she left her job voluntarily because she was sexually harassed. The court found that the unemployment compensation examiner erred in denying her benefits because he used an objective criteria in determining whether the sexual harassment had occurred.

The court ruled that the claimant was warranted in denying herself subjectively an object of sexual harassment and that the hearing examiner should have elicited and relied on evidence of the subjective state of mind of the claimant in reaching a proper determination in the case. Instead, the court found that the examiner's findings "are largely silent on the issue of the impact of her (the claimant's) experiences."[14]

The court looked to the 1980 guidelines on sexual harassment of the Equal Employment Opportunity Commission (EEOC) for guidance on what legal standard an unemployment compensation examiner should apply in deciding a sexual harassment case. The guidelines state in part:

> "Unwelcomed sexual advances, requests for sexual favors, and other verbal or physical conduct of a sexual nature constitute sexual harassment when . . . (3) such conduct has the purpose or effect of unreasonably interfering with an individual's work performance or creating an intimidating, hostile, or offensive working environment."[15]

The court reasoned that the words in the EEOC guidelines ("effect of unreasonably interfering with work performance") suggest a need for an inquiry into the state of mind of the person toward whom the conduct is directed.

The court wrote:

> Concern with the state of mind of the victim obviates the need to pass judgment upon the seriousness or culpabilities or intentions of the harasser.[16]

The court found "judicial vindication" for the EEOC guidelines on sexual harassment in *Bundy v. Jackson,*[17] where the federal appellate court squarely held that sexual harassment not leading to a loss or denial of tangible employment benefits amounts to sex discrimination in the "terms, conditions, or privileges of employment" in violation of Title VII.[18] Furthermore, the *Bundy* court's analysis focused on the psychological and emotional impact on female victims of sexually stereotyped insults and demeaning propositions.

FOOTNOTES

[1] See C.G.S. (Connecticut) Section 31–236(2)(a).

[2] See e.g. *Marz v. Department of Employment Services,* 256 N.W.2d 287 (1977).

[3] See Annotation, "Unemployment Compensation: Harassment or Other Mistreatment by Employer or Supervisor as 'Good Cause' Justifying Abandonment of Employment," 76 ALR 3d. 1089 and "Note, Unemployment Compensation Benefits for Victims of Work-Related Sexual Harassment," 3 HARV. WOMEN'S L.J. 173 (Spring, 1980).

[4] 3 UNEMPLOY. INS. REP. (CCH), Conn. Paragraph 8968 (Conn. Super. Ct., March 13, 1978).

[5] 15 Or. Appp. 454, 516 P.2d 495 (1973).

[6] *Id.* at 459.

[7] *McPherson v. Employment Division.* 285 Ore. 541, 581 P.2d 1381 (1979).

[8] *Prescod v. California Unemployment Ins. Appeals Bd.* 57 Cal.App.3d 29, 127 Cal. Rptr. 540.

[9] See *McCain v. Employment Division,* 17 Or. App. 442, 552 P.2d 1208 (1974).

[10] *Electrical Reactance Corp. v. Unemployment Compensation Board of Review,* 169 Pa. Super. 269, 82 A.2d 277 (1951).

[11] *Grey Moving and Storage Inc. v. Indus. Comm'n,* 560 P.2d 482 (Colo. 1976).

[12] *Uniweld Products, Inc. v. Indus. Relations Comm'n.* 277 So.2d 827 (Fla. App. 1973).

[13] 25 FEP Cases 1647 (1981).

[14] *Id.* at 1648.

[15] 29 C.F.R. Section 1604.11(a).

[16] 25 FEP Cases 1647, at 1649.

[17] 641 F.2d 934, 24 FEP Cases 1155 (D.C. Cir. 1981).
[18] 25 FEP Cases 1647, at 1649.

§5:15. Criminal Law.

Many of the acts of sexual harassment alleged in cases that have been litigated under Title VII are technically also crimes and could be prosecuted under most criminal sexual conduct laws in the country. The U.S. Supreme Court in *Meritor Savings Bank v. Vinson,*[1] recognized that fact when it noted that the acts of sexual harassment alleged there were not only "pervasive but also criminal conduct of the most serious nature."[2]

In *Meritor Savings Bank,* the plaintiff was subjected to forced sexual intercourse with her supervisor. Such extreme sexual conduct can be prosecuted under state law (e.g. sexual assault in the first degree.)[3] But many states also allow prosecution, upon proof of force or threat of force, of "sexual contact" with the victim's intimate parts, i.e. contact with genital area, groin, inner thigh, anus, breast or buttock.[4]

Some victims of sexual harassment pursue civil remedies against their employer in state or federal court and are also involved in the prosecution of the harasser in state criminal court. However, the limitations of criminal prosecution are clear. First, the prosecution of criminal sexual assault cases is handled by the state prosecutor's office. The victim is only the complaining witness in the case. In some states, sexual assault victims have been afforded certain rights including the right to speak at the sentencing hearing.[5] For the most part, victims have little control over charges brought, plea bargaining process and the final sentence that may be given to the defendants.

Second, the successful prosecution of an assailant has limited results. The prosecution is against the individual harasser, the employee who actually sexually assaulted the victim. That defendant, if found guilty, may be sent to prison or placed on probation, but he will not be ordered to pay damages to the victim for the injuries or harm caused. Those kind of damages are only available in the civil arena. In addition, the victim's employer may be held liable in a civil lawsuit for the acts of its supervisors and co-workers as well as failure to have taken action upon complaint of sexual harassment. That same employer cannot be prosecuted in a criminal sexual assault case. Sanctions against an employer for those actions (or failure to act) can only be imposed in a civil case where the court can order back pay for the plaintiff in a Title VII lawsuit or other damages under state law or federal constitutional claims. (See further discussion of damages and relief available in the civil arena in later chapters in this book.)

With the limitations of such criminal remedies and the difficulty of proof of sexual assault "beyond a reasonable doubt" in a criminal trial, many victims of sexual harassment in the workplace do not choose to pursue criminal prosecutions of the harasser.

FOOTNOTES

[1] —U.S.—, 106 S.Ct. 2399, 40 FEP Cases 1822 (1986).

[2] *Id.* at 2406.

[3] C.G.S. (Connecticut) Section 53a–70.

[4] E.g. sexual assault in the third degree, C.G.S. (Connecticut) Section 53a–72.

[5] E.g. C.G.S. (Connecticut) Section 54–91c.

§5:16. Union Remedies.

A major frustration for unionized employees who seek to file grievances because they have been subjected to sexual harassment in the workplace has been the failure of unions to take sexual harassment seriously. Part of that situation has been attributable in the past to insensitivity to the issue on the part of union officials, union stewards and the rank and file members. Education of union leadership and membership on the issue of sexual harassment has increased dramatically across the country and many more union contracts now include "sexual harassment" as a separate grievable offense.

One legal remedy a union member has against a union is to sue the union for breach of the "duty of fair representation." The

National Labor Relations Act, 29 U.S.C. Section 185 imposes this duty of fair representation upon unions. In *Seritis v. Hotel & Restaurant Employees,*[1] the court defined that duty:

> A union has both a statutory and contractual duty of fair representation of workers whose livelihood depends on the Union and if it acts arbitrarily, discriminatorily or in bad faith in failing to represent a member-employee, its conduct is actionable.[2]

The court found that the union breached this duty to two female members who had resisted its executive officer's sexual advances. This official removed one of the women from her job and failed to accord both of them the benefit of the same job placement services given to other union members similarly situated.[3]

In another arena, labor arbitrators generally agree that unwelcome sexual advances and verbal and physical conduct of a sexual nature, as defined by the guidelines on sexual harassment of the Equal Employment Opportunity Commission (EEOC)[4] do constitute just cause for discipline of the harasser by the employer.[5]

Footnotes

[1] 30 FEP Cases 423 (Ca. Sup. Court 1980), *affirmed,* 37 FEP Cases 1501 (Cal. App. 1985).

[2] 30 FEP Cases 423, at 424.

[3] *Id.* at 424–25.

[4] 29 C.F.R. 1604.11(a).

[5] See e.g. *Dayton Power and Light Co.* 80 LA 19 (1982) and *Fisher Foods,* 80 LA 133 (1983).

§5:17. Summary.

Besides being illegal sex discrimination under Title VII, sexual harassment has been also held to be a viable cause of action under several other legal theories. These causes of actions include common-law tort claims for assault and battery, invasion of privacy and intentional infliction of emotional distress. In addition, federal constitutional and statutory actions have been utilized successfully by plaintiffs who have been subjected to sexual harassment. These additional legal claims have been recognized by the courts as supplemental to Title VII claims, although several courts have found that some tort remedies may be barred by state worker's compensation laws.

These claims, along with unemployment compensation benefits and union remedies, provide a full panoply of relief for an employee who has been sexually harassed. These remedies address not only the employment discrimination, but the physical and psychic damages to the person when subjected to sexual harassment. Some relief is limited to compensatory damages as in Title VII, while under other causes of action, damages may include punitive damages. In all, these diverse causes of action provide victims with various avenues of redress in several different legal and administrative arenas.

CHAPTER SIX

Special Litigation Issues in Sexual Harassment Cases

§6:01. Overview.

Sexual harassment cases, by their very nature, often involve issues that do not ordinarily arise in other employment discrimination litigation. For example, evidentiary issues can be dispositive in a sexual harassment case because the credibility and veracity of the witnesses will sometimes determine whether or not the sexual harassment actually occurred. Or the court may have to decide the relevancy of the plaintiff's prior sexual history because of the nature of the acts that she alleged were sexual harassment.

On the other hand, the courts have not always addressed sexual harassment cases in the same way as in any other Title VII case. A classic example is that the courts found a violation of Title VII in racial harassment cases in 1971, but not sexual harassment cases until 1981, when the ruling in *Rogers v. EEOC,*[1] that racial slurs and racial epithets illegally "polluted" the work environment, was followed by the court in *Bundy v. Jackson.*[2] In *Bundy,* the court held that the supervisor had "poisoned" the work environment with "sexually stereotyped insults and demeaning propositions," in violation of Title VII.

While the slowness of the courts to recognize sexual harassment as a Title VII violation was dicussed in the introduction to this book, this chapter will explore some of the issues that arise, especially in sexual harassment cases. Some of these issues, such as damages and credibility determinations, do, of course, arise in other employment discrimination cases. But because of the unique nature of the allegations in a sexual harassment case, special consideration must be given to them in litigation.

FOOTNOTES

[1] 454 F.2d 234, 4 FEP Cases 92, 94 (5th Cir. 1971) *cert. denied,* 406 U.S. 957, 4 FEP Cases 771 (1972).

[2] 641 F.2d 934, 24 FEP Cases 1155 (D.C. Cir. 1981).

§6:02. Evidence.

The evidentiary questions in a Title VII sexual harassment case closely parallel those in criminal prosecutions of sexual assault or rape cases.

In the criminal case, the sexual conduct alleged is usually witnessed by only two people—the victim of the assault and the assailant. In many criminal sexual assault trials, the court determines the innocence or guilt of a defendant by deciding whether the victim or the defendant is most likely telling the truth. In light of that fact, corroborative evidence becomes crucial. In fact it is so important in criminal sexual assault cases that many prosecutors will not bring a case if the possibility of a conviction relies solely on the credibility of the victim's testimony. For that reason, several states today have eliminated the need for corroboration in criminal sexual assault cases by statute.[1]

Consent is also a major issue in criminal sexual assault trials. Many states have changed their laws so that consent is a defense in a criminal sexual assault case, but it is not the victim's burden to show that she did *not* consent to the sexual assault.[2]

Finally, most states have passed statutes, called "rape shield" laws, which make the prior or present sexual history of the victim inadmissible at trial. Some of these laws will allow testimony about the victim's prior sexual history with the defendant if the defendant has raised the issue of consent as a defense at trial.[3]

FOOTNOTES

[1] E.g. Connecticut, C.G.S. Section 53a–68, repealed by P.A. 74–131.

[2] E.g. Connecticut, C.G.S. Section 53a–66, Lack of consent, repealed P.A. 75–619.

[3] E.g. Connecticut C.G.S. 54–86f). See also Berger, "Man's Trial, Woman's Tribulation: Rape Cases in the Courtroom," 77 COL. L.REV. 1 (1977).

§6:03. —Evidence of Plaintiff's Prior Sexual History.

In the civil litigation arena where sexual harassment cases are tried, many of these same issues have arisen and some have been resolved in a similar fashion. The first is the admissibility of the plaintiff's prior sexual history in a Title VII sexual harassment case, which was addressed by the court in *Priest v. Rotary.*[1] The plaintiff objected to defendant's deposition questions about the details of her personal sex life, including the name of each person with whom she had had sexual relationships in the past ten years. When the defendant employer sought a motion to compel the answers, the court magistrate denied and granted the plaintiff's cross-motion for a protective order.

When the defendant appealed that magistrate's ruling, the district court found that as a general rule in federal court civil cases, evidence of an individual's prior acts is not admissible to prove that he or she engaged in similar conduct on a particular occasion. Therefore, the court was clear at the outset "that the information which the defendant seeks to discover regarding the plaintiff's sexual history would be inadmissible to prove her propensity to act in conformity therewith."[2]

It ruled that the evidence sought was not admissible evidence of the plaintiff's "motive" nor was it admissible evidence of "habit."[3] That is, the defendant sought information about the plaintiff's prior sexual history in order to establish her "habit" of living with men "to derive economic benefit from them."[4] The court found the defendant's characterization of plaintiff's conduct as habit "a thinly disguised attempt to seek character evidence"[5] and upheld the magistrate's ruling on the discovery motions. The defendant was prohibited from further inquiry into plaintiff's past sexual behavior.[6]

The court justified its ruling on several grounds.

> Discovery of intimate aspects of plaintiffs' lives, as well as those of their past and current friends and acquaintances, has the clear potential to discourage sexual harassment litigants from prosecuting lawsuits such as the instant one. For those more hearty souls who are determined to have their day in court, it has the potential to annoy and harass them significantly.[7]

Moreover, in reading excerpts from deposition transcripts, the court noted that the "annoyance and discomfort which the plaintiff obviously suffered as a result of defendant's inquiries was unnecessary and deplorable."[8]

> . . . [A] similar state of affairs once confronted victims in criminal prosecutions for rape who often ran the risk of finding their own moral characters on trial during the prosecution of their assailants.[9]

The court explained that since law reform, including Federal Rule of Evidence 412 that excludes evidence of the victim's prior sexual behavior, responded to the plight of the victim in a criminal trial, then "(b)y carefully examining our experience with rape prosecutions . . . the courts and the bar can avoid repeating in this new field of civil sexual harassment suits the same mistakes. . . ."[10]

After *Priest,* the U.S. Supreme Court in *Meritor Savings Bank v. Vinson,*[11] did open up one avenue of inquiry into the plaintiff's sex life. There, in a case in which the plaintiff had prior consensual sexual relations with her supervisor, the Court ruled that testimony of the plaintiff's "dress and personal fantasies" was "obviously relevant."[12]

This evidence was admitted by the district court at trial,[13] but the appellate court in *Vinson v. Taylor,*[14] found "that the testimony had no place in this litigation." It cited *Bundy v. Jackson,*[15] stating that under *Bundy,* a woman does not waive her Title VII rights "by her sartorial or whimsical proclivities."[16]

In *Meritor Savings Bank,* the U.S. Supreme Court found that the appellate court was incorrect in concluding that the plaintiff's voluntariness *vel non* in submitting to her supervisor's sexual advances was immaterial to her sexual harassment claim.[17]

> While "voluntariness" in the sense of consent is not a defense to such a claim, it does not follow that a complainant's sexually provocative speech or dress is irrelevant as a matter of law in determining whether he or she found particular sexual advances unwelcome.[18]

Yet, the Court in *Meritor Savings Bank* was clear that plaintiff's prior consensual sexual relationship with her supervisor is not a defense to a Title VII sexual harassment case. The Court wrote: "The correct inquiry is whether the (plaintiff) . . . by her conduct indicated that the alleged sexual advances were unwelcome, not whether her actual participation in sexual intercourse was voluntary."[19]

No cases since the Court's ruling in *Meritor Savings Bank* have yet elucidated what kind of evidence of a plaintiff's personal life will be allowed in civil sexual harassment cases. Hopefully, courts will be mindful of the considerations set forth in *Priest v. Rotary* above and limit the admissibility of a complainant's prior sexual history as a matter of public policy.

FOOTNOTES

1 98 F.R.D. 755, 32 FEP Cases 1064 (N.D. Calif. 1983).
2 *Id.* at 1066.
3 *Id.* at 1068.
4 *Id.* at 1067.
5 *Id.*
6 *Id.*
7 *Id.* at 1069.
8 *Id.*
9 *Id.* at 1069.
10 *Id.* at 1070.

[11] —U.S.—, 106 S. Ct. 2399, 40 FEP Cases 1822 (1986).
[12] *Id.* at 2407.
[13] *Vinson v. Taylor,* 23 FEP Cases 37 (D.D.C. 1980).
[14] 753 F.2d 141, 36 FEP 1423 D.C. Cir. 1985).
[15] 641 F.2d 934, 944, 24 FEP Cases 1155 (D.C. Cir. 1981).
[16] *Vinson v. Taylor,* 36 FEP Cases 1427, n. 36.
[17] —U.S.—, 106 S. Ct. 2399, at 2407.
[18] *Id.*
[19] *Id.* at 2406.

§6:04. —Evidence of Plaintiff's Past Medical History.

Other evidence requested in discovery in sexual harassment cases and successfully objected to by the plaintiff has included the plaintiff's past medical history and evidence of prior illegal activity.

The plaintiff's medical records were sought by the defendant in *Broderick v. Shad.*[1] The court found the request too broad when it dated back prior to plaintiff's date of hire with the defendant. The request was also irrelevant, even though the plaintiff alleged that as a result of the sexual harassment, she suffered "severe psychological stress," "recurring headaches," and "insomnia."[2]

The court found that the plaintiff did not seek or receive medical treatment for these conditions and that the "focus of this action is not on plaintiff's physical or mental injuries, but rather on the alleged discrimination and harassment" by the employer.[3]

In *Jennings v. D.H.L. Airlines,*[4] the court ruled that the defendant was precluded by the psychotherapist-patient privilege from discovering the records of plaintiff's psychologist. The evidence was sought to prove that plaintiff's complaints of sexual harassment were "caused by her emotional problems and not actual sexual harassment."[5] That is, the defendant argued, the plaintiff was "oversensitive" to the conduct of her co-workers so she thought she was being sexually harassed.

But to disclose the records would likely damage plaintiff's relationship with her psychologist, the court observed, and had she known that the doctor would have to disclose her confidences in a lawsuit, "her trust in (the doctor) . . . doubtless would have been diminished."[6]

Footnotes

[1] 43 FEP Cases 532 (D.D.C. 1987).
[2] *Id.* at 533.
[3] *Id.* at 534.
[4] 34 FEP Cases 1423 (N.D. Ill. 1984).
[5] *Id.* at 1424.
[6] *Id.* at 1425.

§ 6:05. —Evidence of Plaintiff's Prior Illegal Drug Use.

Evidence of prior illegal drug abuse by the plaintiff has also been held inadmissible. In *Crimm v. Missouri Pacific Railroad Co.*,[1] the employer was sued by a former employee who had been discharged for sexually harassing a subordinate. Prior to trial, the defendant employer sought a motion in limine from the court to prohibit the plaintiff from questioning the employee he had harassed about her use of marijuana two or three years before the sexual harassment occurred. The plaintiff opposed the motion, arguing that the evidence was relevant because prior drug use "would indicate unreliability and untruthfulness."[2] The appellate court upheld the district court in granting the motion in limine, as "illegal drug use or transactions, without more, did not show untruthfulness."[3]

Footnotes

[1] 750 F.2d 703 (8th Cir. 1984).
[2] *Id* at 707.
[3] *Id.* at 708.

§6:06. Corroborative Evidence.

Sexual harassment cases are also unique Title VII cases because they often involve close questions of credibility and subjective interpretation of evidence. Here, as in a criminal sexual assault prosecution, corroborative evidence or the lack thereof is likely to be a critical determining factor in how the case is decided by the court.

But in sexual harassment cases, the corroborative evidence is not often eyewitness testimony to the specific acts of sexual harassment the plaintiff alleged happened to her. It is more likely to be testimony from other employees who have also been harassed by the same individual. Several courts have allowed the testimony of these "other women" who have also been harassed.[1]

In *Vinson,* the appellate court chastised the district court for refusing to allow the plaintiff to elicit from other female employees that her supervisor also harassed them. The *Vinson* court saw that *Bundy v. Jackson,*[2] "makes it clear that evidence tending to show (the supervisor's) harassment of other women working alongside Vinson is directly relevant to the question whether he created an environment violative of Title VII."[3] The *Vinson* court goes on to cite *Bundy,*[4] to read that "Such evidence could be critical to a plaintiff's case, for a claim of harassment cannot be established without a showing of more than isolated indicia of a discriminatory environment."[5]

In *Jones v. Flagship Intl.,*[6] the plaintiff argued on appeal that the district court improperly dismissed her allegations of sexual harassment as insufficient to create a hostile work environment. That court understated the "pervasiveness of the sexual harassment she experienced,"[7] because "it failed to take into account sexually harassing incidents reported by other female employees."[8] The appellate court, however, ruled: "Such testimony, though relevant in a class action suit, does not bear on Jones' individual claim of sexual harassment in the absence of evidence that such incidents affected Jones's psychological well-being."[9]

Lack of corroborative evidence can be fatal in a sexual harassment case. In *Hall v. F.O. Thacker Co.,*[10] the district judge did not credit plaintiff's testimony that sexual advances were made of her because that testimony was "virtually uncorroborated."[11] In *Burns v. Terre Haute Regional Hosp.,*[12] the plaintiff's claim was denied when defendant supervisor "vehemently denies the allegations" and there was insufficient corroborative evidence of the plaintiff's allegation.

FOOTNOTES

[1] See *Phillips v. Smalley Maintenance Services,* 711 F.2d 1524, 32 FEP Cases 975, 981 (11th Cir. 1983); *Vinson v. Taylor,* 753 F.2d 1414, 36 FEP Cases 1423 (D.C. Cir. 1985); *Horn v. Duke Homes,* 775 F.2d 599, 37 FEP Cases 228, 230 (7th Cir. 1985). See also *Mays v. Williamson & Sons,* 591 F. Supp 1518, 35 FEP Cases 1868, 1869 (E.D. Ark. 1984), where corroborative testimony was, in fact, eyewitness testimony by a female co-worker as to sexual harassment of plaintiff by her supervisor.

[2] 641 F.2d 934, 24 FEP Cases 1155 (D.C. Cir. 1981).

[3] 753 F.2d 1414, 36 FEP Cases 1423, at 1427.

[4] 641 F.2d 934, at 943 n. 9.

[5] 753 F.2d 1414, at 1427, n. 40.

[6] 793 F.2d 714, 43 FEP Cases 358 (5th Cir., 1986).

[7] *Id.* at 363.

[8] *Id.* at 363, n. 7.

[9] *Id.*

[10] 24 FEP Cases 1499, 1503 (N.D. Ga. 1980).

[11] *Id.* at 1503.

[12] 581 F. Supp. 1301, 37 FEP Cases 1304, 1309 (S.D. Ind. 1983).

§6:07. Credibility of Plaintiff's Testimony.

Besides corroboration, the credibility of the plaintiff's testimony becomes particularly important when the alleged harasser categorically denies the allegations. See *Heelan v. Johns-Manville Corp.,*[1] where plaintiff was most credible despite total denial by defendant supervisor and failure of employer to investigate complaint, and, *Vinson v. Taylor,*[2] where defendant supervisor denied all of plaintiff's charges.

These credibility determinations can be very close and rely on the credibility of each party to the action as well as the credibility of each party's corroborative witnesses on both sides. In *Horn v. Duke Homes,*[3] the appellate court found "the case hinged on a simple credibility determination" and concluded that the harasser's testimony was not credible.[4] The district court judge also credited the plaintiff's testimony which was corroborated by three witnesses.[5]

The court decision in *Wimberly v. Shoney's Inc.*[6] demonstrates the difficulty of this credibility determination in a sexual harassment case. Five female employees brought this action against their supervisor, a restaurant manager. They alleged he sexually harassed them by touching them, making indecent propositions, obscene and lewd comments and profane remarks.[7] The court made several critical credibility determinations including the following:

> Plaintiff testified to several incidents she claimed to be harassment. Plaintiff stated that (her supervisor) . . . once put his arm around her and rubbed her shoulder while he talked to her. She put on no corroborating evidence, and admitted on cross-examination that she did not think the act had sexual connotations. In rebuttal, (the supervisor) testified that the incident "could have happened," and if it did, it was a friendly gesture with no sexual intent on his part.[8]

Ultimately, after examining the claims of each plaintiff and determining the credibility of the witnesses, the court concluded: "There was no credible evidence of continuous, sustained or pervasive sexually oriented misconduct."[9]

In *EEOC v. Domino's Pizza, Inc.*,[10] the district court upheld the magistrate's credibility findings and ruling that sexual harassment, including a forced physical sexual assault of the plaintiff, had indeed occurred. The magistrate found the plaintiff to be "a credible witness," and the defendant supervisor "to be a totally noncredible witness."[11] The court was "particularly unimpressed" with his demeanor on the stand, "his asserted inability" to recall certain events and his "categorical denial" of any sexual suggestions, advances or physical sexual assaults, "especially in light of the plaintiff's apparently accurate awareness of a butterfly tatoo on his leg."[12]

These credibility determinations of the trial judge, beside being dispositive of cases at trial, are given great deference by the appellate court. An appellate court in a civil rights case will respect a finding of fact premised on a credibility choice unless that finding is clearly erroneous.[13] This deference to the trial court is because the trial judge has had the opportunity to observe the demeanor and appearance of all witnesses and make the most valid credibility determination.

Because the trial court's credibility determination is so pivotal in a sexual harassment case, the plaintiff's burden at trial is not only to produce evidence of the sexual harassment, but also credible, corroborated evidence. Thus, credibility is critical when the court decides if the sexual harassment has occurred. It has also been a determining factor when, if the harassment is shown, the court examines the reason that an employer took an action against an employee who alleged the sexual harassment. The court may make a credibility determination in finding that reason was "pretextual," i.e. for a discriminatory purpose. There it is a question of whether the employer's testimony and evidence of its business reason is more credible than the plaintiff's evidence of pretext.[14]

FOOTNOTES

1 451 F. Supp. 1382, 20 FEP Cases, 251, 254 (D. Colo. 1978).

2 23 FEP Cases 37, 39 (D.D.C. 1980).

3 775 F.2d 599, 37 FEP Cases 228, 230 (7th Cir. 1985).

4 *Id.* at 230.

5 *Id.*

6 39 FEP Cases 444 (S.D. Ga. 1985).

7 *Id.*

8 *Id.* at 447.

9 *Id.* at 453.

10 34 FEP Cases 1075 (E.D. Mich. 1983).

11 34 FEP Cases 1075, at 1076.

12 *Id.*

13 See *Danner v. U.S. Civil Service Commission,* 635 F.2d 427, 430–31, 25 FEP Cases 1634 (5th Cir. 1981); *Barnes v. Jones County School District,* 575 F.2d 490, 494, 22 FEP Cases 1519 (5th Cir. 1978).

14 See *Harrison v. Reed Rubber Co.,* 603 F. Supp. 457, 37 FEP Cases 1545 (E.D. Mo. 1985).

§6:08. Defamation Actions Against Complainants.

Like some, but not all, Title VII cases, charges of sexual harassment by an employee and allegations in a sexual harassment lawsuit will contain words and phrases that may be defamatory of the alleged harasser. Since damage to that individual's reputation or good name in the community can be a result of such allegations, several harassers have brought defamation actions against the complainant in a separate action.

There are two reported cases. In *EEOC v. Levi Strauss & Co.,*[1] the EEOC filed an injunction action in federal court to bar a state court action by the alleged harasser against the plaintiff for slander and defamation. The EEOC charged that the filing of the defamation suit violated Title VII because the employee was retaliated against as a result of filing a Title VII complaint.[2] The alleged harasser filed a motion to dismiss the EEOC action in the federal court.

In response, the court found that there is not authority for the proposition that Title VII preempts all state defamation proceedings.[3] The court wrote: "Rather those suits initiated in state court in good faith and as an attempt to rehabilitate the employer's reputation which may have been tarnished by the charges are not necessarily violations of the (Title VII)."[4] Yet, the court denied the alleged harasser's motion to dismiss, finding that the EEOC could establish that the defamation action in state court was filed for improper, i.e. retaliatory purposes and that was a question of fact to be determined by the court.

In *Barnes v. Oody,*[5] two men filed defamation actions alleging they were defamed by two fellow employees who complained to their employer and told co-workers that the plaintiffs had sexually harassed them. The cases, which began in state court, were removed to federal court on motion of the defendants.[6] The plaintiffs had been suspended for 30 days by the employer when it was established that they had engaged in sexual harassment. This determination was by an administrative tribunal in an arbitration proceeding under a collective bargaining agreement.

The district court, on a motion for summary judgment by the defendants, found that the defamation action should be dismissed. It cited the fact that the plaintiffs had a "full and fair" hearing and an opportunity to cross-examine their accusers but the truth of the charges of sexual harassment was established in the administrative tribunal.

The plaintiffs were now collaterally estopped from relitigating the issue of whether the plaintiffs were guilty of sexual harassment in the defamation lawsuit. For that lawsuit, based on the claim that the defendant's allegations of sexual harassment were malicious and false, is barred by the "truth" of the findings of the administrative tribunal, "acting in a judicial capacity."[7]

The courts in both of these cases were mindful of the rights of the plaintiffs to pursue defamation actions in state courts. The reality of the situation is that such defamation actions could deter employees from complaining about sexual harassment and pursuing legal remedies against it. The court in *Barnes* did address whether statements taken during an official investigation of the sexual harassment complaints could be the basis for a state defamation action. The statements were found to have been prepared by the defendants "within the outer perimeter of their lines of duty," and not a proper basis for the defamation action.[8] Such a ruling provides some leeway for an employee to cooperate fully in an in-house investigation of their complaints of sexual harassment without fear of liability in a future defamation action.

Footnotes

[1] 27 FEP Cases 346 (N.D. Ill. 1981).

[2] 42 U.S.C. Section 2000e–3(a).

[3] 27 FEP Cases 346, at 349.

[4]. *Id.* at 350.

[5] 28 FEP Cases 816 (E.D. Tenn. 1981).

[6] *Id.* at 817.

[7] *Id.* at 818.

[8] *Id.* at 819.

§6:09. Damages in a Sexual Harassment Case.

In *Johnson v. Railway Express Agency Inc.,*[1] the U.S. Supreme Court found that Congress created in Title VII "statutory rights against invidious discrimination" in employment and established a "comprehensive scheme for the vindication of those rights."[2] But despite Title VII's range and its design as a comprehensive solution to employment discrimination, the remedies and relief it provides is somewhat limited, particularly in a sexual harassment case. That is one reason that the U.S. Supreme Court ruled that plaintiffs could pursue other claims in addition to a Title VII claim.[3]

In the sexual harassment area, these additional claims have most often been state tort or contract claims although federal constitution and statutory causes of action have also been alleged. (See previous chapter in this book for full discussion of other legal theories of sexual harassment.) What these additional claims do in a sexual harassment case is to broaden the kinds of remedies available to plaintiffs under Title VII.

Under Title VII, a court can award a victorious plaintiff reinstatement, back pay or "any other equitable relief as the court deems appropriate."[4] Injunctive relief is also available if the court finds that the employer has "intentionally engaged . . . in an unlawful employment praclice." That employer can be enjoined from engaging in such practices and "order such affirmative action as may be appropriate."[5] Attorney fees are allowed to the "prevailing party."[6]

In sexual harassment cases, particularly hostile work environment cases where the plaintiff may be fired from her job but still experience illegal sexual harassment, back pay or reinstatement are not always appropriate remedies. The employer could, of course, be enjoined from allowing future harassment in the workplace. But that may be the extent of Title VII remedies for this plaintiff.

Even in cases where the plaintiff has been fired or left her job ("constructive discharge") because of sexual harassment, the court may not find reinstatement an appropriate remedy where illegal sexual conduct has been proven. In *Mays v. Williamson,*[7] the court had serious doubts about ordering reinstatement of plaintiff "since the Defendant is a wholly owned and managed family corporation, and the animosity between the parties was obvious at trial."[8] However, in *EEOC v. Domino's Pizza, Inc.,*[9] the court ordered reinstatement in light of the fact that the supervisor who sexually harassed and physically sexually assaulted the plaintiff "is no longer with defendant corporation."[10] But no injunction relief was ordered in the case because of "the absence of any evidence that anyone other than (this supervisor) . . . made any improper sexual advances or committed any sexually offensive acts."[11]

Beside these remedies of back pay, reinstatement, injunctive relief and attorney fees, the majority of federal courts have construed "equitable relief" to go much further. Courts have precluded any award of damages for emotional harm resulting from a Title VII violation.[12] This is a major problem for a Title VII litigant in a sexual harassment case, although this kind of relief has been sought under state tort and contract claims and federal constitutional and statutory causes of action. For example, in *Phillips v. Smalley Maintenance Services, Inc.,*[13] the plaintiff was awarded under $3,000 in back wages for the Title VII claim, but a jury gave her $10 for common-law battery and $25,000 in compensatory damages for a state law claim of invasion of privacy. In *Rogers v. Loews L'Enfant Plaza Hotel,*[14] the plaintiff sued for common-law torts of invasion of privacy, assault and battery and infliction of emotional distress. Her damages requested were $500,000 in compensatory and punitive damages and the court found that she was entitled to pursue these damages before a jury.

Thus, the plaintiff who has been sexually harassed and suffered emotional harm must look to state common-law tort remedies and other federal statues that allow punitive and other damages for emotional harm. But this means that a plaintiff must be the victim of the kind of egregious harassment and physical assaults that establishes a *prima facie* case of infliction of emotional distress, invasion of privacy or assault and battery in order to expect relief on this basis from the courts. (See *Rogers* for a good discussion of the *prima facie* case elements for each of these torts.)

FOOTNOTES

[1] 421 U.S. 454 (1975).
[2] *Id.* at 457–58.
[3] 421 U.S. 454 (1975).
[4] 42 U.S.C. Section 2000e–5g.
[5] *Id.*
[6] 42 U.S.C. Section 2000e–5(k).
[7] 591 F. Supp 1518, 35 FEP Cases 1869 (E.D. Ark. 1984).
[8] *Id.* at 1871.
[9] 34 FEP Cases 1075 (E.D. Mich. 1983).
[10] *Id.* at 1077.
[11] *Id.*
[12] *Henson v. City of Dundee,* 682 F.2d 897, 29 FEP Cases 787 (11th Cir. 1982). See *Bundy v. Jackson,* 641 F.2d 934, 24 FEP Cases 1155, 1162, n. 12 (D.C. Cir. 1981) for a listing of cases.
[13] 711 F.2d 1524, 32 FEP Cases 975 (11th Cir. 1983).
[14] 526 F. Supp. 523, 29 FEP Cases 828 (D.D.C. 1981).

§6:10. Summary.

Special litigation issues that are unique to a sexual harassment case include the admissibility of certain kinds of evidence about the plaintiff, the availability of damages for emotional harm and the possibility of defamation actions against the employee who has complained of sexual harassment.

These issues are unique to sexual harassment cases because of the personal nature of the allegations made against an alleged harasser and the injuries that can be inflicted in sexual harassment but not other employment discrimination cases. The courts have been responsive to issues of this nature and the results have often been sensitive to the interests of a victim of sexual harassment without restricting the ability of the employer to present its case to the court.

CHAPTER SEVEN

The Answer Yet To Come In Sexual Harassment Cases

§7:01. Overview.

It was only 11 years ago that a federal court first decided that sexual harassment was sex discrimination under Title VII of the Civil Rights Act of 1964.[1] Since then, state and federal courts have decided many cases of sexual harassment, but the jurisprudence of sexual harassment cases is indeed still very young.

In 1986, the U.S. Supreme Court decided its first sexual harassment case in *Meritor Savings Bank v. Vinson.*[2] Its decision, perhaps unwittingly, laid out the agenda of legal issues in sexual harassment cases that courts will certainly face in the next decade. For the issues raised were the important and difficult ones, some that appear uniquely in sexual harassment cases.

In concluding this book that has explored many of the important legal issues in sexual harassment cases, it is instructive to set forth again what answers are yet to come in sexual harassment litigation.

FOOTNOTES

[1] *Williams v. Saxbe*, 413 F. Supp. 654 (D.D.C. 1976).

[2] —U.S.—, 106 S. Ct. 2399, 40 FEP Cases 1822 (1986).

§7:02. The Propositions of Meritor Savings Bank.

The U.S. Supreme Court in *Meritor Savings Bank*[1] clearly held that:

1. "When a supervisor sexually harasses a subordinate because of a subordinate's sex, that supervisor discriminates on the basis of sex."[2] That is generally taken to affirm a cause of action for *quid quo pro* sexual harassment.
2. "Nothing in Title VII suggests that a hostile environment based on discriminatory sexual harassment should not be likewise prohibited. A plaintiff may establish a violation of Title VII by proving that discrimination based on sex has created a hostile or abusive work environment."[3]
3. "For sexual harassment to be actionable, it must be sufficiently severe or pervasive 'to alter the conditions of [the victim's] employment and create an abusive working environment'."[4]
4. "The correct inquiry is whether respondent by her conduct indicated that the alleged sexual advances were unwelcome, not whether her actual participation in sexual intercourse was voluntary."[5]
5. "There is no *per se* rule against admissibility" of evidence about respondent's dress and personal fantasies.[6]
6. "The Court of Appeals erred in concluding that employers are always automatically liable for sexual harassment by their supervisors . . . For the same reason, absence of notice to an employer does not necessarily insulate that employer from liability."[7]
7. ". . . [M]ere existence of a grievance procedure and a policy against discrimination coupled with respondent's failure to invoke that procedure, must insulate petitioner from liability."[8]

FOOTNOTES

[1] —U.S.—,106 S. Ct. 2399, 40 FEP Cases 1822 (1986).

[2] *Id.* at 2404.

[3] *Id.* at 2405.

[4] *Id.* at 2406.

[5] *Id.*
[6] *Id.* at 2407.
[7] *Id.* at 2408.
[8] *Id.* at 2408–2409.

§7:03. Issues Remaining After Meritor Savings Bank.

While the U.S. Supreme Court offered guidance on the above issues, some of its holdings were not definitive or broad enough to provide litigators with clarity on the following questions.

1. How does a plaintiff prove sexual harassment was unwelcome?

While the U.S. Supreme Court stated that the "correct inquiry is whether the plaintiff by her conduct indicated that the sexual advances were unwelcomed," the question remains as to what evidence plaintiff must offer to show the sexual harassment was unwelcomed. In the past, lower courts had ruled that the unwelcomeness of acts of sexual harassment should be judged by a subjective standard, that is, from the victim's perception. Recently one appellate court since *Meritor Savings Bank* used a "reasonable person" standard to decide if acts of sexual harassment are unwelcome to the victim. The dissenting judge in that case vehemently criticized that standard, charging that it would most likely mean that sexual harassment will be viewed "from ingrained notions of reasonable behaviors fashioned by the offenders, in this case, men."[1] That judge proposed a "reasonable women" standard, because research shows that men and women differ in their view of sexual harassment in the workplace. Would the Supreme Court find appropriate either standard? The answer to this question is yet to come. (See Chapter 1 of this book for a more complete discussion of when sexual harassment is unwelcome.)

2. What evidence of plaintiff's "dress and personal fantasies" is relevant to the inquiry of whether the sexual harassment was "unwelcome"?

The Court's holding in *Meritor Savings Bank* that there is no *per se* rule against admissibility of evidence of the plaintiff's "dress" and "personal fantasies," is troublesome because it portends allowing testimony of a plaintiff's personal sex life in sexual harassment lawsuits. It also implies that somehow a woman asks for sexual harassment because of what she wears or fantasizes about. While proof that the sexual harassment was "unwelcome" is clearly an important element that a plaintiff must establish in her *prima facie* case, how the Court envisions that "dress" and "personal fantasies" evidence is relevant to this inquiry is not clear. (See Chapter 5 of this book for a more complete discussion of this evidence issue.)

3. What is the "definitive" rule on when an employer is strictly liable for the acts of supervisors that create a hostile work environment?

While the Court declined the parties' invitation in *Meritor Savings Bank* to issue a definitive rule on employer liability, this issue remains a controversial one. Circuit Courts of Appeal are split on the question and the Supreme Court in *Meritor Savings Bank* only offered minimal guidance. That guidance was that employers are not always "automatically" liable for sexual harassment but the "absence of notice does not insulate an employer" from liability. Court decisions since *Meritor Savings Bank* are not forging ahead to answer this question of strict liability, but harkening back to earlier, less controversial liability rules. This question remains to be definitively answered. (See Chapter 3 of this book for a more complete discussion of employer liability issues.)

4. What does it mean that an employer has an internal grievance procedure for employees to make complaints about sexual harassment? Does an employee have to use it to give an employer proper notice of a complaint? If an employer takes immediate corrective action on such a complaint, can it escape liability of those acts?

The Court in *Meritor Savings Bank* touched on some of the issues when it ruled that the "mere" existence of a grievance procedure, and the failure of the plaintiff to use it, do not insulate the employer from liability. But that begs the question of does some particular kind of grievance procedure, coupled with the plaintiff's use of it *and* immediate corrective action by the employer absolve the employer of responsibility? Some lower courts have found that immediate corrective action does negate employer liability, while others have said it only mitigates damages. Clarity on employer liability is also awaited here. (See Chapter 4 of this book for a more complete discussion of employer defenses.)

Footnotes

[1] *Rabidue v. Osceola Refining Co.*, 42 FEP Cases 631, 642 (6th Cir. 1986).

§7:04. Other Remaining Issues in Sexual Harassment Litigation.

Other legal questions are not posed within the facts of *Meritor Savings Bank* but are also outstanding issues in the area of sexual harassment litigation.

The most controversial issue is the cause of action for sexual favoritism. This claim, which has been allowed under Title VII by the EEOC guidelines on sexual harassment and several court decisions, relies on an employee complaint that she has been denied a tangible job benefit because another less qualified candidate has received it who has provided sexual favors to the decisionmaker. While recognizing this cause of action, the courts have also required that the plaintiff have proof of a sexual relationship between the less qualified candidate and the decisionmaker. What proof is required and why are unanswered questions that need more legal thinking and analysis. (See Chapter 1 of this book for a more complete discussion of this cause of action for sexual favoritism.)

The most improbable, yet possible, question the courts might still face in sexual harassment cases is whether a female employee who is harassed by a supervisor who also harasses male employees will be a victim of sexual discrimination. Early reported cases of sexual harassment as well as some recent decisions still contend that a bisexual supervisor in such a scenario would negate the discrimination on the basis of sex. Some courts have definitely eliminated the possibility that such a case would appear or be interpreted in that way, but others still see the case looming on the horizon to challenge the theory of sex discrimination underlying sexual harassment cases.

One clear thought in sexual harassment cases that will hold true in the future is that the real key to combating sexual harassment is prevention. The EEOC guidelines on sexual harassment state the case the best.

> Prevention is the best tool for the elimination of sexual harassment. An employer should take all steps necessary to prevent sexual harassment from occurring, such as affirmatively raising the subject, expressing strong disapproval, developing appropriate sanctions, informing employees of their right to raise and how to raise the issue of harassment under Title VII, and developing methods to sensitize all concerned.[1]

FOOTNOTES

[1] 29 C.F.R. 1604.11(f).

Index

D

E

J

L

M

N

P

Q

R

S

V

W